*"The lamps are going out all over Europe;
we shall not see them lit again in our lifetime."*

— Sir Edward Grey,
British Foreign Secretary,
August 4, 1914

Published in Great Britain and
the United States of America in 2016 by
CASEMATE PUBLISHERS
10 Hythe Bridge Street, Oxford OX1 2EW, UK
and
1950 Lawrence Road, Havertown, PA 19083, USA

ISBN 978-1-61200-348-1

A CIP record for this book is available from the British Library

Printed in the Czech Republic by FINIDR

For a complete list of Casemate titles, please contact:

CASEMATE PUBLISHERS (UK)
Telephone (01865) 241249
Fax (01865) 794449
Email: casemate-uk@casematepublishers.co.uk
www.casematepublishers.co.uk

CASEMATE PUBLISHERS (US)
Telephone (610) 853-9131
Fax (610) 853-9146
Email: casemate@casematepublishing.com
www.casematepublishing.com

Text editor: Nikolai Bogdanovic

The extract from Vera Brittain's *Testament of Youth* is included by
permission of Mark Bostridge and T.J. Brittain-Catlin, Literary Executors
for the Estate of Vera Brittain 1970.

Extracts from *The War Poems of Siegfried Sassoon* and *Memoirs of an
Inventory Officer*. © Siegfried Sassoon, by kind permission of the Estate of
George Sassoon.

"... and the world went dark"

An Illustrated Interpretation of the Great War

Steven N. Patricia

CASEMATE | uk
Oxford & Philadelphia

PREFACE

"World War I", "The Great War", or "The War to End All Wars" was fought by at least 16 countries, on seven fronts and at sea, for over four years by over 65 million combatants. The lasting effects of this conflict were to completely change the political structure and the social and economic fabric of Europe, the Middle East and Africa. They set the stage for World War II and the subsequent military conflicts, police actions and terrorist insurgencies of the entire following 20th century.

The Centennial Years of the Great War are here and interest in this subject will likely grow. However, in the US in particular, the distance in time and place may still cause many to question the relevance of this foggy history. At best, some may realise that they had a past relative who served overseas, and may even know some of their stories. Family histories tend to keep some information alive, but the scale and intensity of the war is lost to most.

Many primary documents exist in the form of letters, diaries, testimonials and military records. Personal accounts represented by the letters home should not be relied on as a source of factual history. Millions of letters were written by all combatants during the war. Soldiers in the First World War were not allowed to write about certain things like their position, the conditions, suspected enemy movements or plans for attacks. All the letters sent home would be proofread by censors to prevent unsettling or confidential information being forwarded to families and possibly intercepted by the enemy. In fact, if a soldier was too distressed or fatigued there was always the "Field Service Post Card". All of the participating countries used this and it was composed of a series of simplistic and unemotional phrases that could be crossed out if not applicable.

NOTHING is to be written on this side except the date and signature of the sender. Sentences not required may be erased. If anything else is added the post card will be destroyed.

[Postage must be prepaid on any letter or post card addressed to the sender of this card.]

I am quite well.

I have been admitted into hospital
{ sick } and am going on well.
{ wounded } and hope to be discharged soon.

I am being sent down to the base.

I have received your { letter dated 20/0/1918.
{ telegram „ ———
{ parcel „ ———

Letter follows at first opportunity.

I have received no letter from you
{ lately
{ for a long time.

Signature }
only } Rev.

Date 20/2/18

Wt. W1568-R1619.18530 8000m. 6-17. C. & Co., Grange Mills, S.W.

Field Service Post Card

I have based most of my information on diary accounts. Such writings were usually not intended for the public review and as a result are more likely to reflect the writer's inner feelings. Some of the following accounts are truly powerful and emotional, and are so well written that they conjure strong imagery.

This book is not primarily about the causes of the Great War or the political, economic, military strategies, etc. Such comprehensive studies and portrayals have been done and will be done by others. It is about war and the human condition; war and the tragedy of war.

The words collected here are from those who were there. The artwork is derived from historic photographic imagery for its accuracy and relevance. The images are my interpretations from emotional impulses of those stories and observations. Hopefully, these interpretations will impart a sense of respect for all of those young, old, hopeful, fearful and desperate participants in an unprecedented world conflict that happened so long ago...

" All blood runs red "

— Phrase painted on the side of the plane flown by
Eugene Ballard, the first African-American military pilot

INTRODUCTION
The Forces that Led to War

Although the assassination of Austrian Archduke Franz Ferdinand in Sarajevo on June 28, 1914 is seen as the spark that ignited the Great War, longer term factors had been at play. The origins of the conflict lay in the complex network of military and political alliances forged throughout the 19th and early 20th centuries.

Russia, Austria and Prussia had entered a "Holy Alliance" in the wake of the Napoleonic Wars. Following the unification of Germany in 1871, Prussia was absorbed into the nascent German nation and in the years that followed Austria-Hungary, Russia and Germany continued to attempt to strengthen their political ties. Tension soon arose between Austria-Hungary and Russia over Bosnia-Herzegovina (under the former's control since the late 1870s), leading to the signing of the 1879 Dual Alliance between Austria-Hungary and Germany. Italy would join them in 1882, creating what became known as the Triple Alliance.

Seeking to avoid any future bi-frontal war, German efforts to find common ground with Russia continued. However, the enthronement of Wilhelm II as Kaiser witnessed a more muscular attitude to the East in the 1890s. This was a factor leading to the Franco-Russian Alliance of 1891–93.

Great Britain also witnessed an end to her neutrality in Europe in this period. Several agreements, known collectively as the Entente Cordiale, were signed on April 8, 1904, reducing Franco-British antagonism, and in 1907 the Anglo-Russian Convention was ratified. These agreements developed into what became known as the Triple Entente. Europe was thus clearly divided into two opposing blocs.

Under the terms of the Treaty of Berlin (1878), **Austria-Hungary occupies Bosnia-Herzegovina**. The major European powers recognise Serbia as a sovereign state.

A decade of successive crises heightens the tensions between the Great Powers. Events in Morocco, the Balkans, Libya, the Dodecanese and territories of the fracturing Ottoman Empire all cause lasting damage to relations between the major players in the coming war.

Germany and Russia realign themselves politically. Germany, a new imperial power and in the ascendant following victory in the Franco-Prussian War, becomes closer to Austria-Hungary, while Russia realigns itself with France.

On July 30, Tsar Nicholas of Russia orders mobilisation; Kaiser Wilhelm orders preparations to enter Luxembourg and Belgium as a preliminary move towards invading France – the Schlieffen Plan. Austria-Hungary orders a general mobilisation on July 31. France follows on August 1.

Great Britain ends its policy of **"Splendid Isolation"**, which saw minimal involvement in European affairs and a strong desire to "not to entangle itself with any single or monopolising alliance with any [nation]."

The July Crisis: on July 28, Austria-Hungary declares war on Serbia. At 1.00am the next day, the Austrian monitor S.M.S. *Bodrog* bombards Belgrade. Russia orders a partial mobilisation along the Austro-Hungarian border.

1914

SARAJEVO, SERBIA
JUNE 28, 1914

Germany declares war on Russia (August 1), then France (August 3) and Belgium (August 4). Britain declares war on Germany in return.

On August 6 Austria-Hungary declares war on Russia. On August 12, France and Britain declare war on Austria-Hungary.

A **naval arms race**, chiefly between Great Britain and Germany, develops. German concern over the strength of Britain's navy causes Wilhelm II to order a sizeable expansion of the High Seas Fleet; the Royal Navy reciprocates. France and Russia also start to spend more on their respective miltary forces.

Archduke Franz Ferdinand of Austria and his wife Sophie are assassinated in Sarajevo on June 28 by Gavrilo Princip. Austria-Hungary issues an ultimatum to the Kingdom of Serbia, demanding it respect the Great Powers' decision regarding Bosnia-Herzegovina.

The seemingly minor event of the assassination of Archduke Franz Ferdinand of Austria by Serbian separatists in Sarajevo on June 28, 1914 was the spark that set the tinderbox of Europe alight. General outrage resulted, and with the approval of Germany, Austria-Hungary attacked Serbia. Russia, aligned with Serbia, was reluctantly provoked into living up to its self-proclaimed role of protector of all Slav nations and mobilized against Austria and Germany. France too began to prepare for war. Despite diplomatic efforts by various key individuals from all the great powers, Germany declared war on Russia, and two days later, on the flimsy and later disproved excuse of border violations, on France too.

Britain had no desire to enter the conflict, but the invasion of Belgium and France, Britain's allies, and the now overriding perception of Germany as the power-hungry aggressor with no respect for innocent civilians and international law quashed all dissent, so Britain was also drawn into the fight.

The decisions that led to war had been made by only a few men, the ruling monarchs and leaders of government. These leaders managed to convince the people of their respective countries that their nation was the victim of intrigue and conspiracy, and promised a "short war", a noble endeavour that would result in a more moral, liberated society. Optimism and a patriotic fervour were the order of the day.

"Had there been a Bismarck in Germany, a Palmerston or Disraeli in Britain, a Roosevelt in America, or a Clemenceau in authority in Paris, the catastrophe might, and I believe would have, been averted"

— David Lloyd George,
British prime minister,
1916–1922

"The German people must be made to see that we have to attack because of our enemies' provocation. Things must be so built up that war will seem as a deliverance from the great armaments, the financial burdens, the political tensions. We must also prepare for war financially, though without awakening financiers' suspicions... If we are attacked, we shall do as our brothers did, a hundred years ago [against Napoleon]... Let us remember that many provinces of the old German Empire, such as the County of Burgundy and much of Lorraine, are still in French hands; that thousands of our German brothers groan under the Slav yoke in the Baltic. Germany must regain what formerly she lost."

— Helmuth Johannes Ludwig von Moltke
German chief of staff, in a report to the Emperor,
March 13, 1913

Germany, Britain and Russia all had heads of state who were cousins through the lineage of Britain's Queen Victoria and Prince Albert. "Willie" (Kaiser Wilhelm) was certain that "Nicky" (Tsar Nicholas II) and "Georgie" (King George V) would never interfere. Wilhelm was greatly disappointed, especially by Britain's declaration of war, and this led to furious hatred in Germany of the "treacherous" British.

King George V

Tsar Nicholas II

Kaiser Wilhelm II

Declarations of War: 1914-1918

"When the cannon is still at night, I hear the groans and the death rattle of the wounded who have not been picked up... Quite often the Prussians dispatch our wounded soldiers with a lance thrust or a blow with the butt of a musket. I know what I am talking about for I have seen it."

— Letter of a French solider between
Aisne and Marne, September 26, 1914

1914

JULY
28th: Austria on Serbia

AUGUST
1st: Germany on Russia
3rd: Germany on France
4th: Germany on Belgium
Britain on Germany
5th: Montenegro on Austria
6th: Austria on Russia
Serbia on Germany
8th: Montenegro on Germany
12th: France on Austria
Britain on Austria
23th: Japan on Germany
25th: Japan on Austria
28th: Austria on Belgium

NOVEMBER
2nd: Russia on Turkey
Serbia on Turkey
5th: Britain on Turkey
France on Turkey

1915

MAY
23rd: Italy on Austria

AUGUST
21st: Italy on Turkey

OCTOBER
14th: Bulgaria on Serbia
15th: Britain on Bulgaria
Montenegro on Bulgaria
16th: France on Bulgaria
19th: Russia on Bulgaria
Italy on Bulgaria

1916

MARCH
9th: Germany on Portugal
15th: Austria on Portugal

AUGUST
27th: Romania on Austria
28th: Italy on Germany
Germany on Romania
30th: Turkey on Romania

1917

APRIL
6th: U.S.A. on Germany
7th: Panama on Germany
Cuba on Germany

JUNE
27th: Greece on Austria, Bulgaria,
Germany & Turkey

JULY
22nd: Siam on Germany & Austria

AUGUST
4th: Liberia on Germany
14th: China on Germany & Austria

OCTOBER
26th: Brazil on Germany

DECEMBER
7th: U.S.A. on Austria
10th: Panama on Austria
16th: Cuba on Austria

1918

APRIL
23rd: Guatemala on Germany

MAY
8th: Nicaragua on Germany
& Austria
23rd: Costa Rica on Germany

JULY
12th: Haiti on Germany
19th: Honduras on Germany

America in World War I

America remained neutral for over half the war, in accordance with George Washington's famous warning against involvement in European affairs, and this was supported by the great majority of the American people. Although sympathies lay with the Allies, Woodrow Wilson did not believe at first that America's interests were threatened, and he successfully ran for re-election under the slogan "He kept us out of the war". He also attempted to mediate between the warring countries.

But gradually opinion changed, and incidents such as the execution of the British nurse Edith Cavell, the sinking of the *Lusitania*, and the Zimmerman note – in which Germany proposed that in the case of war between Germany and the United States, Mexico should be induced to declare war on the U.S.A. – did much to alter the public mood. But it was the declaration by the Germans of unrestricted submarine warfare on January 31, 1917 that was the key factor in the U.S. joining forces with the Allies; as soon as American ships were sunk, war was declared.

The first troops of the American Expeditionary Force, often known as "Doughboys" arrived in June 1917, but did not make it to the front until a few months later.

The Great War Tragedy
The Players

Great Britain and her Colonies

" Our hearts beat with enthusiasm. A kind of intoxication takes possession of us. My muscles and arteries tingle with happy strength. The spirit is contagious. Along the line track walkers wave to us. Women hold up their children. We are carried away by the greeting of the land, the mystery that the future holds, the thought of glorious adventure, and the pride of being chosen to share it."

— Andre Fribourg,
The Flaming Crucible, 1918

8,410,000
mobilised

3,190,325
casualties

" The brutality and inhumanity of war stood in great contrast to what I had heard and read about as a youth"

— Reinhold Spengler,
1916

United States

4,355,000 mobilised
364,800 casualties

"No commander was ever privileged to lead a finer force; no commander ever derived greater inspiration from the performance of his troops."

— John J. Pershing

"He had come to America, haven of peace and liberty, and it, too, was joining the slaughter, fighting for the big capitalists. There was no peace for men, only murder, cruelty, brutality."

— James T. Farrell

Germany

11,000,000 mobilised

7,142,558 casualties

"I am not going to take any unnecessary chances. I want to die well and not be killed in some accident or die of sickness – that would be terrible, a tragic anticlimax. I haven't lived very well but I am determined to die well. I don't want to be a hero...

"Thank God I am going to have the opportunity to die as every brave man should wish to die – fighting – and fighting for my country as well. That would retrieve my wasted years and neglected opportunities."

— Diary of John MacGavock Grider, 1917

France

8,410,000 mobilised
6,160,800 casualties

" It's a terrible tragedy. And yet, in its
details, it's great fun. And – apart from the
tragedy – I've never felt happier or better in
my life than in those days in Belgium"

— Rupert Brooke,
Christmas 1914

Japan

800,000 mobilised
1,210 casualties

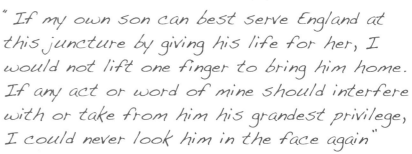

" If my own son can best serve England at
this juncture by giving his life for her, I
would not lift one finger to bring him home.
If any act or word of mine should interfere
with or take from him his grandest privilege,
I could never look him in the face again"

— Mrs Berridge, in *The Morning Post*,
September 30, 1914

Soldiers are dreamers;
when the guns begin
They think of firelit homes,
clean beds and wives.

— Siegfried Sassoon, *Dreamers*

Belgium

267,000 mobilised
93,061 casualties

Austria-Hungary

7,800,000 mobilised
7,020,000 casualties

Turkey

2,850,000 mobilised
975,000 casualties

Greece

230,000 mobilised
17,000 casualties

Bulgaria

1,200,000 mobilised
266,919 casualties

Montenegro

50,000 mobilised
20,000 casualties

" ...These are men whose minds the Dead have ravished,
Memory fingers in their hair of murders,
Multitudinous murders they once witnessed.

" By choice they made themselves immune
To pity and whatever moans in man
Before the last sea and the hapless stars;
Whatever mourns when many leave these shores;
Whatever shares the eternal reciprocity of tears.

" Men marched asleep. Many had lost their boots
But limped on, blood-shod. All went lame; all blind;
Drunk with fatigue; deaf even to the hoots
Of tired, outstripped Five-Nines that dropped behind.

" ...Tonight, His frost will fasten on this
        mud and us,
            Shriveling many hands, puckering
            foreheads crisp.
                The burying-party, picks and shovels
                in their shaking grasp,
                    Pause over half-known faces.
                    All their eyes are ice,
                        But nothing happens."
                                    — Wilfred Owen

Serbia

707,343 mobilised
331,106 casualties

Russia

12,000,000
mobilised
9,150,000
casualties

Italy

5,615,000 mobilised
2,197,000 casualties

Portugal

100,000 mobilised
33,291 casualties

Romania

750,000 mobilised
535,706 casualties

" Every soldier was supposed to have not just the regular amount of 120 cartridges, but much more. Sometimes, every one of us had up to 300 cartridges. They weigh almost one pud [16.4 kg]. On those long marches, these heavy loads bothered the men. To remedy the situation they threw the cartridges into the ditches where no one picked them up... When the soldiers rested for the night somewhere, they took the rifle apart and used the butts to build a fire. I have done this myself several times, to warm us up and to boil water for tea...

" ...So now, during the retreat from Galicia, many of the soldiers go into a fight without weapons. They wait for the dead and the wounded to acquire a rifle."

— J. Oskine, 1915

ACT I
THE WAR IN THE AIR

"So it was that the war in the air began. Men rode upon the whirlwind that night and slew and fell like archangels. The sky rained heroes upon the astonished earth. Surely the last fights of mankind were the best. What was the heavy pounding of your Homeric swordsmen, what was the creaking charge of chariots, besides this swift rush, this crash, this giddy triumph, this headlong sweep to death?"

— H. G. Wells, *The World Set Free*, 1914

It was still very early days for aviation at the time of World War I, and the concept of using airplanes to wage war was a radical idea, greeted with scepticism. The Wright Brothers' first successful flight had taken place on December 17, 1903, and in the eleven years since, numerous aircraft were developed. In fact, more than 70 different types of aircraft were used in World War I. These early planes were basic; made of wood and fabric they had enough power to lift a single pilot and in some cases one passenger too.

The most important job for pilots at the beginning of the war was reconnaissance. As the value of the intelligence gained was immediately apparent, the need to defeat the "observation" flights became paramount and by the war's first anniversary aviators were in constant danger. Ground fire from small arms and artillery proved ineffective until the advancements in anti-aircraft fire, called "Archie" or "flak". Reconnaissance pilots also carried their own small arms with which to shoot down the enemy, and even threw grenades, bricks or grappling hooks (none of which, incidently, were very effective). Russian ace Alexander Kazakov even dangled explosives below his plane in an unsuccessful but admirable attempt to bring down an opponent.

The use of the machine gun in aircraft became practical in 1915 when Anton Fokker, a Dutch aircraft designer, perfected his "interrupter gear", which synchronized the guns with the engine to keep them from firing into the propeller. A host of other technical developments took place between 1914 and 1918, the most significant of which was the use of the rotary engine which produced a high power to weight ratio and made aircraft much more maneuverable.

Innovations such as these opened the door to direct aerial combat. However, the designs of these planes required an enormous amount of skill to fly them. New air recruits typically received only 3-5 hours of actual flight training, and coupled with bad weather and mechanical failure this led to a huge number of accidental deaths. The life expectancy of a pilot was approximately 2 weeks.

"Aces" were pilots credited with striking down at least five enemy planes in combat. Fascination with fighter pilots dates from 1915 when the world began to take notice of aerial warfare. With a world war subjecting it to mass slaughter, the public craved heroes. With the new and adventurous fighter pilots battling it out in seemingly equal contests, came the much looked-for idols. Manfred von Richthofen, also known as the "Red Baron", is considered the most successful ace of the war with 80 confirmed victories. He was shot down and killed near Amiens in 1918.

" If I should come out of this war alive, I will have more luck than brains."

— Captain Manfred von Richthofen,
a.k.a. the Red Baron

Willy Omer Coppens de Houthuist
Belgian Military Aviation
37 confirmed kills

Godwin Brumowski
Luftfahrtruppen
Austria-Hungary
35 confirmed kills

William "Billy" Avery Bishop
Royal Air Force
Canada
72 confirmed kills

Francesco Baracca
Corpo Aeronautico Militaire
Italy
34 confirmed kills

Arthur Henry Cobby
Australian Flying Corps
29 confirmed kills

René Fonck
Aéronautique Militaire
(France)
75 confirmed kills

Alexander Kazakov
Imperial Russian Air Force
20 confirmed kills

Edward Vernon Rickenbacker
U.S. Army Air Service
26 confirmed kills

Manfred von Richthofen
Luftstreitkräfte
Germany
80 confirmed kills

The "Aces"
The Great War's Greatest Airmen

Balloons

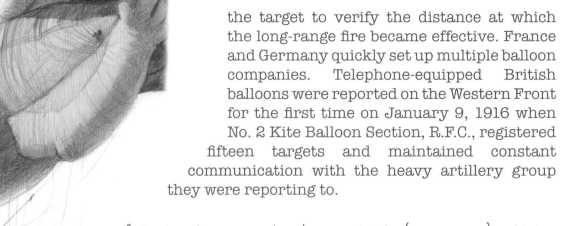

The balloon is the oldest military aircraft, with the first war-related flight taking place in 1794. The design of early balloons restricted their use, as observers bouncing around in any wind stronger than a gentle breeze became airsick and often found it impossible to remain focused on enemy targets. But German design improvements a century later led to the re-introduction of balloons – zeppelins, or airships – into the military sphere.

" I cannot get over it. The Zeppelin is in the zenith of the night, golden like the moon, having taken control of the sky. Our cosmos has burst; the stars and the moon blown away, the envelope of the sky burst out, and a new cosmos has appeared."

— D. H. Lawrence

When the war on the Western Front settled into the trenches, indirect artillery fire began to dominate the battlefield and artillery commanders needed a view of the target to verify the distance at which the long-range fire became effective. France and Germany quickly set up multiple balloon companies. Telephone-equipped British balloons were reported on the Western Front for the first time on January 9, 1916 when No. 2 Kite Balloon Section, R.F.C., registered fifteen targets and maintained constant communication with the heavy artillery group they were reporting to.

" But when you look up at the ' sausage ' shining in the sunshine three or four miles away, and know that there are eyes in it which can see you and report your movements to the nearest battery, you begin to be uncomfortable. They have so much advantage of you, those eyes in the sky"

— *Adelaide Register*, October 16, 1916

Reconnaissance from balloons enabled far greater accuracy with artillery fire, with targets far behind the front lines accessible for the first time. Filled with helium or hydrogen, they were tethered to a steel cable attached to a winch.

" It was a dream, conjecturable as heaven, resembling no life we knew. We were trained with one object – to kill. We had only one hope – to live. When it was over we had to start again. I do not complain of this. It was a fine introduction to life."

— Cecil Lewis

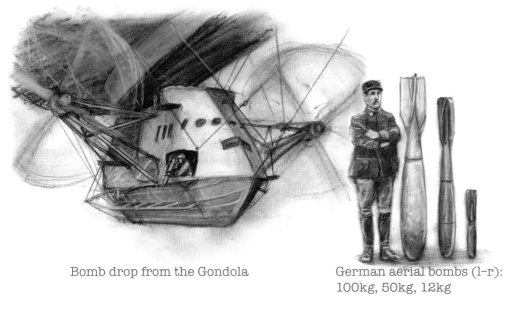

Bomb drop from the Gondola

German aerial bombs (l-r):
100kg, 50kg, 12kg

Loading ordinance under a British Avro 529

But lighter-than-air aircraft also brought a new, more deadly threat. As early as the 1860s, Count Ferdinand von Zeppelin sought to develop a weapon able to win a war. The zeppelin, an airship capable of travelling long distances carrying heavy loads brought the prospect of attack from the air to civilian populations, military infrastructure and industry far behind the front lines.

The first strategic aerial bombardments of the war were conducted by Germany in 1915 against urban targets in Great Britain. On January 19, 1915, two zeppelins dropped twenty-four high-explosive bombs on Great Yarmouth, Sheringham and King's Lynn. Bombing raids by airships increased until 1917 when British air defences improved. By the end of the war, 51 raids had been carried out, in which nearly 6,000 bombs were dropped, killing 557 people and injuring over 1,300.

By 1917, the use of zeppelins proved to be too costly and inefficient, and the so-called "heavy bombers" became the preferred method of attacking strategic targets. These could carry considerably larger payloads and fly much greater distances than previous airplanes.

Soldiers prepare "flak"
to fire at enemy aircraft

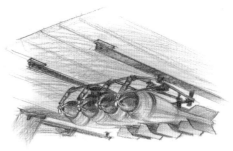

Bombs racked and
ready for delivery

Heavy Bombers

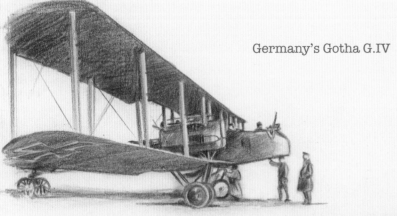

Germany's Gotha G.IV

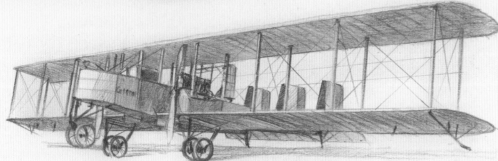

Italy's Caproni Ca.3

Britain's Handley Page H. P. O./400

" I was a member of a Royal Air Force unit, nineteen years of age. The infantryman was one in a tiny circle of pals, each circle but one wavelet in a huge sea. His was a hard life – mud and blood and losing chums, and ever conscious of being but a cog in a mighty and soulless machine.

" We, on the other hand, were neither wavelets nor cogs. We were a small family of officers living in decent huts, partaking of decent meals, sleeping in clean pyjamas, and generally living in comfort for eighteen hours of the twenty-four. In the remaining six we might plunge into the welter of war in which the infantryman lived, but we did our particular job in a clean atmosphere in a clean way, and when we killed or were killed it was done in that same inevitable and highly respectable manner. The infantryman looked up from his rat hole and said, with his hair on end, that he wouldn't have our risky job for anything, while we looked down on his muddy wastes and said, ' Poor devils!`, and flew home to a hot dinner served on a clean tablecloth while he cut his fingers opening bully-beef tins.

" The family were, of course, occasionally bereaved, and we talked rather awkwardly at dinner and avoided each other's eyes. But coffee, smokes, and piano quickly saved us from overmuch thought."

— Rev. John H. W. Haswell, *Everyman at War*, 1930

"Here above us, there is a man twenty metres above the earth, imprisoned in a wooden frame, and defending himself against an invisible danger which he has taken on of his own free will..."

— Franz Kafka

"The air was our element, the sky our battlefield. The majesty of the heavens, while it dwarfed us, gave us, I think, a spirit unknown to sturdier men who fought on earth. Nobility surrounded us. We moved like spirits in an airy loom, where wind and cloud and light wove day and night long the endless fabric of the changing sky."

— Cecil Lewis

"I decided to dive at her... firing a burst straight into her as I came. I let her have another burst as I passed under her and then banked my machine over... and pumped lead into her for all I was worth... As I was firing, I noticed her to begin to go red inside like an enormous Chinese lantern. She shot up about two hundred feet, paused, and came roaring down straight on to me before I had time to get out of the way. I nose-dived for all I was worth, with the zeppelin tearing after me... I put my machine into a spin and just managed to corkscrew out of the way as she shot past me, roaring like a furnace..."

— British Lt. W. J. Tempest,
October 1915

"I hate to shoot a Hun down without him seeing me, for although this method is in accordance with my doctrine, it is against what little sporting instincts I have left."

— James McCudden, V.C., R.F.C., 1917

The Diary of
John MacGavock Grider
R.A.F. Pilot, 1892–1918

May 14th, 1918

I gave my new plane a work-out in the air today. I put it level just off the ground and it did 130. Then I went up high and did a spinning tail slide. Nothing broke so I have perfect confidence in it...

The cockpit looks like the inside of a locomotive cab. In it is a compass, airspeed indicator, radiator thermometer, oil gauge, compensator, two gun trigger controls, synchronized gear reservoir handle, hand pump, gas tank gauge, two switches, pressure control, altimeter, gas pipe shut-off cocks, shutter control, thermometer, two cocking handles for the guns, booster magneto, spare ammunition drums, map case, throttle, joystick and rudder bar. That's enough for any one man to say grace over.

It has two guns; one Vickers and one Lewis. The Vickers is mounted on the fuselage in front of your face and fires thru' the propeller. The Lewis is mounted on the top wing and fires over the top of the propeller. It has two sights: a ring sight and an Aldis telescope sight. I set both sights and both guns so that they will all converge at a spot two hundred yards in front of the line of flight.

When you aim, what you really do is aim the plane and the guns take care of themselves. The Vickers has a belt of four hundred rounds and the Lewis has a drum of one hundred and we carry three spare drums. The Vickers is the best gun by far. Of course, I can't resist the temptation to add a few devices of my own and have also put a cupboard and a shelf in for spare goggles, machine gun tools, cigarettes, etc. I am also decorating my cockpit. When you are in the air for two or three hours at a time, you get awfully bored...

July 1st, 1918
I hear that Matthews is now a member of the sadder-but-wiser club. He dove straight down on a two-seater and the observer didn't do a thing but shoot the front end of his plane full of holes. He got back to the lines but cracked up and lit on his neck. These boys will learn some day that one two-seater can lick one scout any time unless the scout can stick under his blind spot. The long ones have a hole in the bottom of the fuselage and they can shoot down at you and these new ones have a double tail and are so short that the observer can stand up and fire right down on you while the pilot simply pulls up in a stall... And you can't take them from a front angle because the observer can traverse his guns over the top of the upper wing... If you want to go to heaven, the easiest way I know is to dive on a two-seater. We all do it but the percentage of gentlemen who get cured of it is mounting.

July 4th, 1918
They say Archie [flak, or anti-aircraft fire] is the most useless thing in the war, but that machine gun fire from the ground is greatly to be feared. That's what got Richtofen. I came back to-day and found a couple of bullet holes in my rudder. Machine guns only carry up to about twenty-five hundred feet but Archie can go higher than we can...

Archie has a funny sound. A burst near you sounds like a loud cough and as soon as you hear it you start zig-zagging. It won't hurt you – but it does mean that the battery has your range and the next one is sure to come closer unless you fool

him and sideslip, zoom, turn, or throttle down. Then he fires where you should have been but weren't.

He's easy to fool. The best thing to do is to change your course twenty degrees every twelve seconds. That gives you time to get out of the way of the one that's coming at you and doesn't give the gunners time to get your deflection for the next shot.

February 22nd, 1918
...Montgomery was killed when the pilot fell out of the front seat in an Ak. W. in a loop. Montgomery was in the back seat and crawled up into the front cockpit and just had his hands on the controls when it crashed. Think of watching the ground coming up at you for two or three minutes while you wiggle up the fuselage. Makes my blood run cold!

The Huns use shrapnel which bursts black and the Allies use high explosive which bursts white. There is an Austrian naval battery at Middlekirke that bursts pink. Scared me to death the first time I saw it.

March 10th, 1918
Heard today that Ludwig was killed flying an S. E. He got into a spin close to the ground.

July 7th, 1918
The Fokkers are giving us hell. A flight lost two men yesterday and Webster got all shot up again. He doesn't consider the day well spent unless his mechanics have a few holes to patch... John Goad is dead. He was shot down in flames flying a Bristol Fighter. When the flames got too hot he turned the machine upside down and jumped.

July 23rd, 1918

I have learned many things, especially that discretion is the better part of valor. And in this game, not only the better part, but about ninety-nine per cent of it. When there are more than two Huns above you and your immediate vicinity is full of lead, well, my boy, it is high time to go home. Never mind trying to shoot down any of them. Go home and try again tomorrow. How do you go home? You are far in Hunland and you are lonesome. If you put your nose down and run for home you will never live to tell it.

March 20th, 1917
Cush Nathan killed. He was flying an S. E. and the wings came off at 5,000 feet. He went into the roof of a three-storey house and they dug him out of the basement. A real fine fellow. I liked him. So did everybody...

First you must turn, bank ninety degrees and keep turning. They can't keep their sights on you. Watch the sun for direction. Now there's one on your right - shoot at him. Don't try to hit him - just spray him - for if you try to hold your sight on him you'll have to fly straight and give the others a crack at you. But you put the wind up him anyway and he turns. Quick, turn in the opposite direction. He's out of it for a moment. Now there's another one near you. Turn again, you are between them and the lines. Now go for it, engine full on, nose down. Two of them are still after you - tracer getting near again. Pull up, zoom and sideslip and if necessary, turn and spray them again. Now make another dive for home. If your wings don't fall off and you are gaining on them, pull up a little.

Ah, there's Archie, that means they are behind you - woof - that one was close - you now have another grey hair

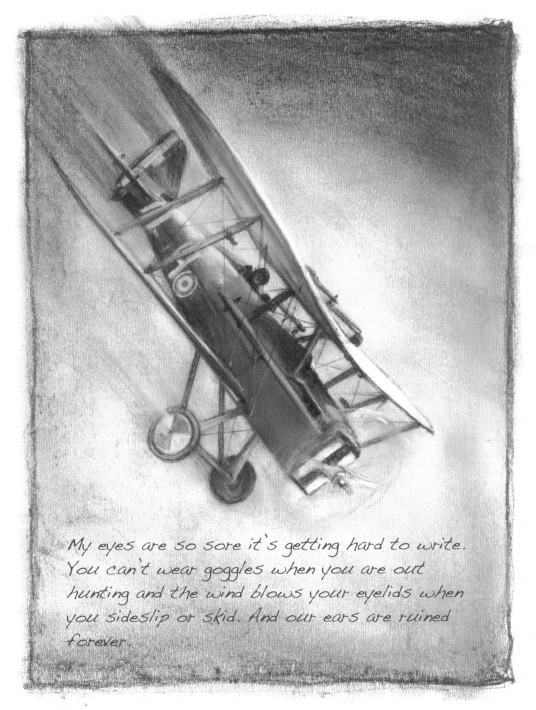

My eyes are so sore it's getting hard to write. You can't wear goggles when you are out hunting and the wind blows your eyelids when you sideslip or skid. And our ears are ruined forever.

– they've been watching you – better zig-zag a bit. He's a joke compared to machine guns. You dodge him carefully and roll in derision as you cross the lines and hasten home for tea.

July 28th, 1918
McCudden the great has been killed. He'd just gotten back from England and had been flying with a light load over there. He forgot that he had four bombs on now and full load of ammunition and he pulled up too steep.

It's not the fear of death that's done it. I'm still not afraid to die. It's this eternal flinching from it that's doing it and has made a coward out of me. Few men live to know what real fear is. It's something that grows on you, day by day, that eats into your constitution and undermines your sanity. I have never been serious about anything in my life and I know that I'll never be otherwise again. But my seriousness will be a burlesque, for no one will recognize it.

Here I am, twenty-four years old, I look forty and I feel ninety. I've lost all interest in life beyond the next patrol. No one Hun will ever get me and I'll never fall into a trap, but sooner or later I'll be forced to fight against odds that are too long or perhaps a stray shot from the ground will be lucky and I will have gone in vain... I haven't a chance, I know.

Last week I actually got frightened in the air and lost my head. Then I found ten Huns and took them all on and I got one of them down out of control. I got my nerve back and came back home and slept like a baby for the first time in two months.

I know now why men go out and take such long chances and pull off such wild stunts. No discipline in the world could make them do what they do of their own accord. I know now what a brave man is. I know now how men laugh at death and welcome it...

This war gets more dangerous every day. And now this colonel has gotten bloodthirsty and wants some balloons. He's welcome to them. It means in addition to other things that we will carry

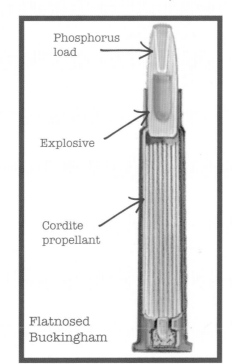

Phosphorus load

Explosive

Cordite propellant

Flatnosed Buckingham

flatnosed Buckingham to set the balloons on fire and if we get shot down in Hunland they will shoot us at once on the ground if they find any of it in our guns.

...Today we ran into five Fokkers at 15,000 feet. We climbed up to 20,500 and couldn't get any higher. We were practically stalled and these Fokkers went right over our heads and got between us and the lines. They didn't want to dogfight but tried to pick off our rear men.

Gosh, it's unpleasant fighting at that altitude. The slightest movement exhausts you, your engine has no pep and sputters; it's hard to keep a decent formation, and you lose 500 feet on a turn. We put up the best fight of our lives but these Huns were just too good for us. Cal got a shot in his radiator and went down and Webster had his tail plane shot to bits and his elevator control shot away.

I got to circling with one Hun, and it didn't take me long to find out that I wasn't going to climb above this one. He began to gain on me and then he did something that I've never heard of before. He'd be circling with me and he'd pull around and point his nose at me and open fire and just hang there on his prop and follow me around with his tracer. All I could do was to keep on turning the best I could. If I'd straightened out he'd have had me cold as he already had his sights on me. But this fellow just hung right there and sprayed me with lead like he had a hose. All I could do was watch his tracer and kick my rudder from one side to the other to throw his aim off.

This war isn't what it used to be...

John MacGavock Grider died in aerial combat at the end of August 1918, shot down by a German plane 20 miles behind the German lines. He was found by the Germans and given a decent burial; his grave was later discovered by the Red Cross.

"The heavens were the grandstands and only the gods were spectators. The stake was the world, the forfeit was the player's place at the table, and the game had no recess. It was the most dangerous of all sports and the most fascinating. It got in the blood like wine. It aged men forty years in forty days. It ruined nervous systems in an hour."

— Elliot White Springs, *Warbirds: The Diary of an Unknown Aviator*

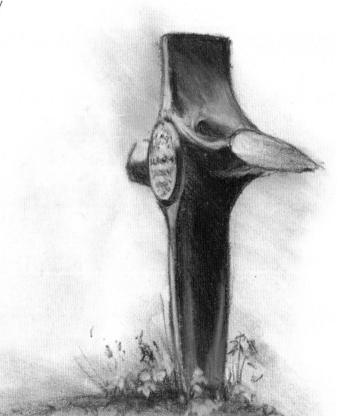

ACT II
THE WAR AT SEA

" I saw a torpedo speeding toward us, and immediately I tried to change our course, but was unable to manoeuvre out of its way. There was a terrible impact as the torpedo struck the starboard side of the vessel, and a second torpedo followed almost immediately. This one struck squarely over the boilers."

— Captain William Thomas Turner of the cruise liner *Lusitania*, sunk on May 7, 1915 by a German submarine with the loss of 1,198 lives, including 128 American civilians. The tragedy strongly influenced America's entry into the war in 1917.

Britain had been the world's dominant naval force since the Napoleonic Wars, but in the years leading up to 1914, it became locked in a naval arms race with Germany. The resulting tension was, many believe, a significant factor in the outbreak of war.

The British launch of H.M.S. *Dreadnought* in 1906 brought a new generation of ships to the fore; her design – with powerful steam turbine engines and ten 12-inch guns – made all previous warships obsolete. Germany immediately responded by building its own dreadnoughts and many other countries followed suit. By 1914 Germany had an impressive fleet. Although smaller, France, Italy, Russia, Austria-Hungary, Japan and the United States all had modern fleets with at least some dreadnoughts and submarines.

Yet for the first two years of the war the British, whose senior officers trained during the age of sail, concentrated their efforts on a defensive strategy, thinking that the size of the fleet was its key advantage in retaining control of the North Sea. Great sea battles between large surface fleets were rare; instead the Allies protected trade routes, developed anti-submarine devices and established and maintained a trade blockade of Germany and her allies, preventing merchant ships supplying raw materials and food.

Those who longed for action got their wish on May 31–June 1, 1916 when the two fleets finally met in direct combat at the Battle of Jutland off the coast of Denmark. This was to prove to be the only major naval battle of the war; both sides claimed victory and the outcome has been controversial ever since; the Germans inflicted heavier losses, but the British remained the dominant naval force.

The war at sea was critically important for the overall outcome of the war. The naval blockade significantly weakened Germany; but they were masters of another new form of technology that almost reversed this situation: submarines.

Underwater Warfare

Soon after the outbreak of war, Britain imposed an economic blockade on Germany and the Central Powers. Both in home waters and across the globe, Allied patrols began to intercept merchant shipping destined for Germany. Germany retaliated with a cruiser-led campaign against merchant shipping destined for the Allied Powers.

Both Britain and Germany had developed submarine fleets from the early 1900s. The submarines of both sides conducted widespread operations in the Baltic, North Sea, Atlantic, Mediterranean and Black Seas. The first U-boat attack on Royal Navy warships took place in August 1914.

By mid-1915 the threat to merchant shipping from the regular warships of the German navy had vanished, and the duty of

disrupting commerce was handed to the U-boat fleet, which could sink merchant ships without warning. This in turn forced the Allies to develop more effective anti-submarine measures. The rules laid down in sections 6, 7 and 11 of the Hague Convention of 1907 were soon abandoned by both sides, leading to several temporary periods of unrestricted warfare against commercial shipping later in the war.

" I expected to be excited but was not a bit; it's hard to express what we did feel like, but you know the sort of feeling one has when one goes in to bat at cricket and rather a lot depends upon you doing well and you're waiting for the first ball; well, it's very much the same as that – do you know what I mean? A sort of tense feeling waiting for the unknown to happen, and not quite knowing what to expect; one does not feel the slightest bit frightened."

— Letter by a British sub-lieutenant, aged 19, to another, aged 17, both unknown

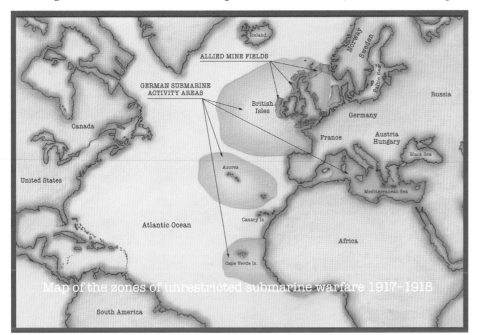

Map of the zones of unrestricted submarine warfare 1917–1918

The Allied Response

80ft ELCO sub chaser boat manufactured in the U.S. for Britain

The Royal Navy developed different methods to counter the threat posed by U-boats. Harbour defences were improved by the addition of barriers, wire nets and mine nets, notably at Scapa Flow in the Orkneys. Aircraft and coastal airship patrols were sent out to look for submarines. The highly secret Q-ships – armed vessels disguised as merchant ships – were used to lure German U-boats to the surface before destroying them at close range. Hydrophones also helped Allied shipping to detect the presence of U-boats in open water. A regular system of transatlantic convoys, where Royal Navy warships would accompany gathered merchant vessels in their journeys to and from Britain, was established in mid-1917, further reducing the number of sinkings. The British Admiralty commissioned the U.S. firm Elco to produce over 500 motor launches for anti-submarine coastal patrol work. These armed vessels entered service in late 1916.

A variety of contact mine and physical barriers were laid across the Dover Straits, the North Channel and the Adriatic Sea. Minefields were also laid by both sides in enemy waters in an attempt to disrupt shipping lanes. A total of 48 German submarines were sunk by Allied mines in the Great War.

The development of the Type D depth charge in 1916 added a new way to destroy a submarine. It consisted of high explosives within a barrel casing, which would explode when the charge reached a certain depth in the water. At first, the depth charges were rolled off the rear of the ships and into the water, but by 1918 special devices called "Y guns" had been developed to project the depth charges through the air and into the sea, creating a wider blast area.

Destroyers screening a convoy

The cruiser *Akashi*, Admiral Kozo Sato's flagship in the Mediterranean

In 1917, the Admiralty introduced "dazzle" painting (a type of naval camouflage) as a direct response to U-boat attacks. These paint schemes relied on the use of strongly contrasting blocks of colour within a pattern to distort the outlines and shape of a vessel. By October 1918 thousands of British and American ships had been camouflaged this way.

The entry of the United States into the war in April 1917 increased the number of anti-submarine vessels available to the Allies. By this stage, the Kaiser's U-boats had once again returned to a policy of sinking Allied merchant shipping without warning. In March 1917 the Imperial Japanese Navy sent a special force, including the armoured cruiser *Akashi*, to help protect Allied shipping in the Mediterranean.

Late-war U-boat operations were made more difficult by widespread mutinies among crews of the German surface fleet, brought on by popular unrest in Germany over food and material shortages caused by the highly effective Allied blockade. On October 20, 1918, the Kaiser recalled all U-boats to port. A month later, Germany's entire U-boat fleet surrendered to the Royal Navy.

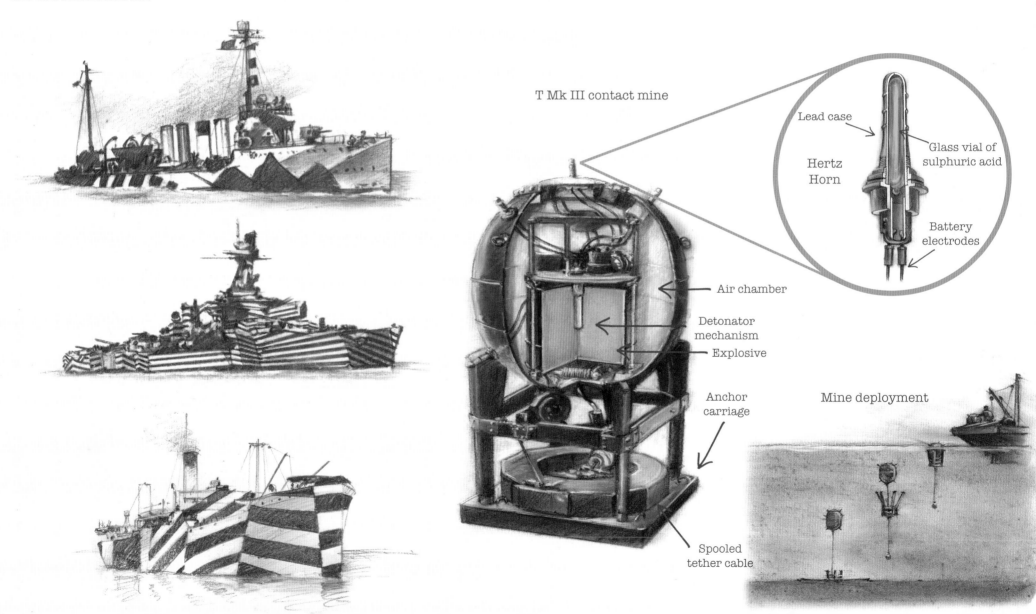

T Mk III contact mine

Lead case

Glass vial of sulphuric acid

Hertz Horn

Battery electrodes

Air chamber

Detonator mechanism

Explosive

Anchor carriage

Spooled tether cable

Mine deployment

Contemporaneous with the contact mine was the depth charge...

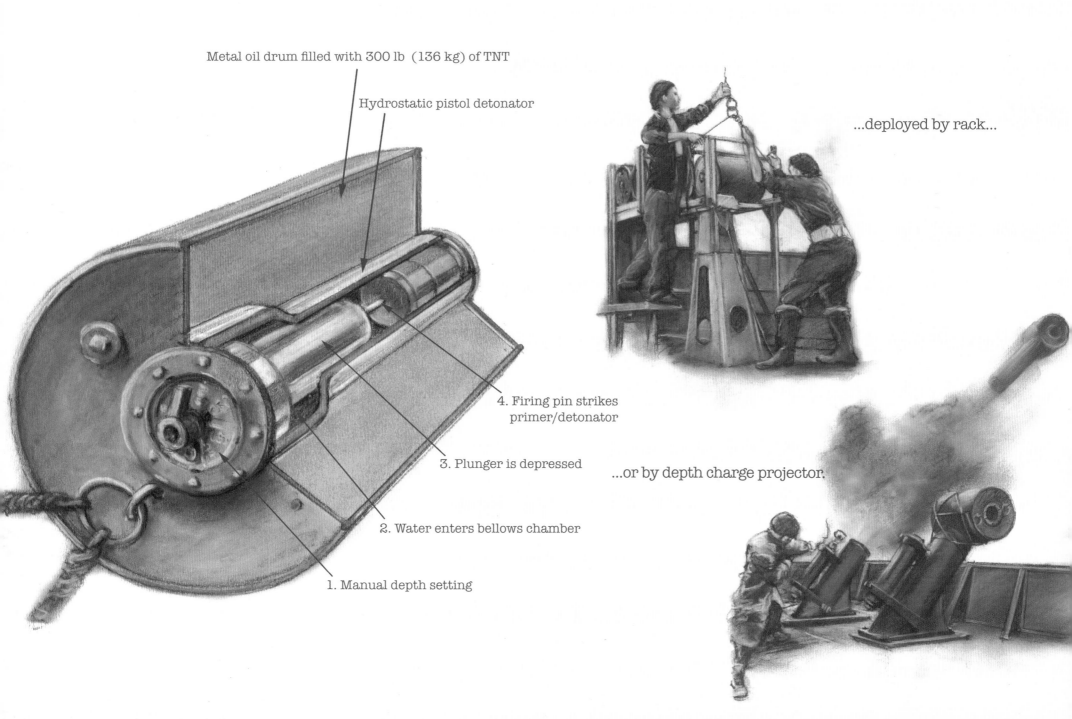

Metal oil drum filled with 300 lb (136 kg) of TNT

Hydrostatic pistol detonator

...deployed by rack...

4. Firing pin strikes primer/detonator

3. Plunger is depressed

...or by depth charge projector.

2. Water enters bellows chamber

1. Manual depth setting

Troop Transport Ships

The ships used for transport were owned by steamship companies, requisitioned by the government who outfitted the ships to meet their new wartime role. On a New Zealand convoy of ten ships travelling from Wellington to Egypt, the authorities somehow squeezed in almost 8,500 soldiers and 4,000 horses, along with the ships' crews and stores.

Conditions for the men varied depending on the weather and the age of the ship, but many were angered by seeing how much better officers lived and ate.

Officers organised physical training programmes, inoculations, lectures and target practice sessions to keep the troops occupied, while keeping an eye out for gambling and smoking on deck at night.

Fights on board were common, sometimes organised by officers for the entertainment of the rest, others more private, vicious affairs.

In the Indian Ocean the heat drove men to sleep on the upper decks. Many horses died – and a few men.

" Our sailing was suspicious as we slipped away at night,
   They corked up all the funnels and they doused each vagrant light,
   As we slipped away to Europe with water, wind, and steam,
   To sail the grand old ocean in the fall of `17".

— Unknown

Hospital Ships

During the Great War, campaigns such as Gallipoli meant there was a pressing need for large hospital ships. Many were requisitioned, and these were ostensibly protected by the Hague convention of 1907, but Allied hospital ships remained targets of German attack.

Perhaps the best known hospital ship was the sister-ship of the *Titanic*, H.M.H.S. *Britannic*, one of the finest vessels of her era, and at the time the largest ship in the world in active service. Requisitioned in 1915, she could carry over 3,300 casualties and had a medical staff of 52 doctors, 101 nurses and 336 orderlies, as well as a crew of 675.

Although *Britannic* was thought to be even more unsinkable than *Titanic*, on November 21, 1916 off the coast of Greece disaster struck when the ship was rocked by a large explosion caused by striking a mine. She sank in 55 minutes, and while 1,036 passengers and crew were rescued, 30 lives were lost. Most of the casualties were in two lifeboats that were pulled into the still-turning propellers:

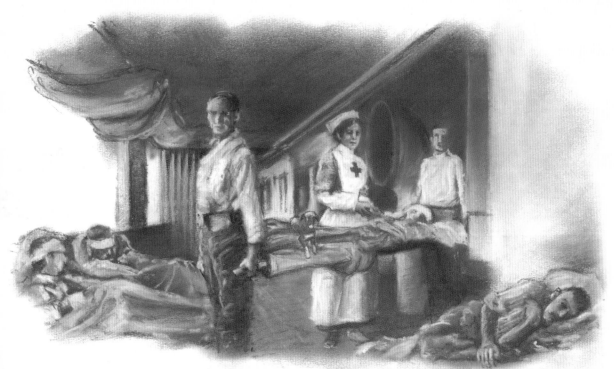

" ...every man jack in the group of surrounding boats took a flying leap into the sea. They came thudding from behind and all around me, taking to the water like a vast army of rats... I turned around to see the reason for this exodus and, to my horror, saw Britannic's huge propellers churning and mincing up everything near them – men, boats and everything were just one ghastly whirl."

— Violet Jessop, a nurse aboard H.M.H.S. *Britannic*

May 17

"I reach the clearing station – everywhere on the narrow beach are numbers of wounded awaiting their removal to the Hospital Ship. Many are gasping out their lives before they can be transferred to the boats. We are towed from ship to ship; always the same reply, 'Full up' – eventually we manage to get aboard one.

May 18

"This is not a proper hospital ship, there is only accommodation for 150 wounded – we have on board some 500 or 600, and the filth is awful. I request to be put on as orderly, for though I am weak with fever and am delirious at night, at least I have the use of my limbs."

May 20

"I have got my two patients up on deck; the atmosphere down there is simply frightful and every thing filthy. One of my cases is a man called Dench, he has been shot in the head and is both deaf and dumb."

May 22

"On deck 6.30 am. Patients are lying here just as they were when they left the trenches, with all the filthy and blood-soaked clothes still upon them. I must get them washed somehow..."

— Signaller Ellis Silas, May 1915

Naval Mascots

Cats were perhaps the most popular mascots aboard ship. They were relatively self-sufficient and earned their keep by abating rodent problems. Of course almost any animal could prove to be a perfect mascot...

Pig

Cat

Raccoon

Goat

Dog

Sinking a British Ship

An eyewitness account by Baron Spiegel von und zu Peckelsheim, commander of German submarine SM *U-32*

On the occasion in question everything went as calculated. The steamer could not see our cautious and hardly-shown periscope and continued unconcerned on its course... I saw the captain walking on his bridge, a small whistle in his mouth. I saw the crew cleaning the deck forward... I saw with amazement - a shiver went through me - a long line of compartments of wood spread over the entire deck, out of which were sticking black and brown horse heads and necks.

Oh heavens, horses! What a pity, those lovely beasts! But it cannot be helped, I went on thinking. War is war... "Torpedo ready!" I called down into the Centrale. Everyone on board held his breath. "Let go!" A light trembling shook the boat - the torpedo was on its way. Woe, when it was let loose! There it was speeding, the murderous projectile, with an insane speed straight at its prey. I could accurately follow its path by the light wake it left.

"Twenty seconds", counted the mate whose duty it was to calculate the exact time elapsed after the torpedo was fired until it exploded.

"Twenty-two seconds!" Now it must happen - the terrible thing! I saw the people on the bridge had discovered the wake which the torpedo was leaving, a slender stripe. How they pointed with their fingers out across the sea in terror; how the captain, covering his face with his hands, resigned himself to what must come. And next there was a terrific shaking so that all aboard the steamer were tossed about and then, like a volcano. arose, majestic but fearful in its beauty, a two-hundred meter high and fifty-meter wide pillar of water toward the sky. A terrible drama was being enacted on the hard-hit sinking ship. It listed and sank toward us.

From the tower I could observe all the decks. From all the hatches human beings forced their way out, fighting despairingly... Panic stricken, they thronged about one another down the stairways, fighting for the life-boats, and among all were the rearing, snorting, and kicking horses... Then another explosion resounded, after which a hissing white wave of steam streamed out of all the ports. The hot steam set the horses crazy, and they were beside themselves with terror – I could see a splendid, dapple-grey horse with a long tail make a great leap over the ship's side and land in a lifeboat, already over crowded – but after that I could not endure the terrible spectacle any longer...

— Baron Spiegel von und zu Peckelsheim

"Suddenly the entire ship is roughly shaken. The colossus heaves far over, and everything that is not fixed is upset... The first direct hit! The torpedo pierces the fore part of the ship. Its effects are terrible. Iron, wood, metal, parts of bodies, and smashed ships' implements are all intermixed, and the electric light, by chance spared, continues to shine upon this sight."

— Trooper Reginald C. Huggins,
on the sinking of the S.S. *Arcadian* in 1917

"So far the great ship had stood firm, as if anchored. We noticed now that she had a definite list to starboard. The angle grew steeper, and then suddenly her bow dropped, her stern lifted, and next she slid to the bottom like a diver. It was as though a living thing had disappeared beneath the waves. We watched her, open-mouthed, a tightness at our hearts. We missed the comfort of her presence, we felt the tragedy of her surrender. It was more than human."

— Albert Kinross,
on the sinking of
a passenger ship

" It is difficult to describe my sensations during the minute or so following. Down and still further down, I was dragged by the suction till it seemed that I must soon touch bottom. I was spun round with great rapidity and swirled about in an alarming manner.

" I held my breath and closed tightly both eyes and mouth, until forced by bursting lungs to take in air, I opened my mouth, getting a large helping of Aegean Sea.

" My mind was functioning normally. I can recollect that I had quite decided that H.M. Army was about to lose one live cavalryman. And though I cannot justly claim to being more courageous than my neighbour, it is curious that having made up my mind that my name would shortly appear in the casualty lists, I was not the least bit afraid... I can give no reason. I was young, eighteen at that time, having declared a false age on enlistment, and naturally I had no overwhelming desire to provide provender for the denizens of the deep.

" At last, however, I came with a rush to the surface, and was violently ill for some time. Glancing at my wristlet watch, I found it had stopped. The time was 5.45 p.m. Large numbers of drowned, the survivors, and a quantity of wreckage were close by me."

— Trooper Reginald C. Huggins,

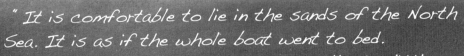

"*During the night we dropped down to the bottom of the ocean...*

" *It is comfortable to lie in the sands of the North Sea. It is as if the whole boat went to bed.*

" *Soon we were sitting, four men in all, at a little, nicely decorated table, cutting into the steaming platter and drinking out of small seidels a magnificent sparkling wine. The past day's events had to be moistened a little with the best we had. This was our custom when the fortunes of war smiled graciously on us... During this time we raised our glasses and drank toasts to one another and to the beautiful U-boat.*

"' *What an original idea for an artist!*' *said our engineer, who was poetically inclined, as he leaned back in his chair staring thoughtfully at the ceiling.*

"' *One can imagine a cross section of the boat showing our room at the North Sea's yellowish sand bottom... In here four feasting, happy officers around a little table on which a warm electric light is shining... Above – water, water, water – water to the height of a church steeple and, over it all, the glittering heavens full of stars and a small silver-white piece of the moon.*

"' *If I were a painter I should immediately start with this motive for a picture... one should in reality propose such a motive to an artist*'."

— Baron Spiegel von und zu Peckelsheim

ACT III
THE WAR ON LAND

" It seems to me as if we stand before the enemy released from everything that has formerly bound us; we stand entirely free there, death can no longer sever our ties too painfully."

— In *War Letters of Fallen Students*, 1936

The Great War was fought on land on many different fronts, often simultaneously. The territorial consequences saw national borders redrawn, newly independent nations created and restored, and colonial spoils shared out among the victors.

Some of the earliest fighting took place in Serbia in late July 1914, when Austria-Hungary invaded Serbia. In Macedonia, the Salonika Front was opened by the Allied Powers to aid Serbia in the autumn of 1915, with a multinational force fighting against German, Austro-Hungarian and Bulgarian armies. In Africa, German colonial territories in the west, east and south-west all witnessed fighting early in the war.

The Western Front occupied the borders between France, Germany and neighbouring countries. Following a full year of inconclusive engagements, a lengthy period of static trench warfare ensued. On the Eastern Front Russia and Romania fought against Austria-Hungary, Bulgaria, the Ottoman Empire and Germany. The front stretched from the Baltic Sea in the north to the Black Sea in the south.

The Gallipoli Campaign, launched in 1915, briefly brought fighting to Ottoman territory in the Dardanelles, in an attempt to control a key Allied sea passage to Russia. After eight months' fighting, the campaign was abandoned and the Allies withdrew in humiliation.

From 1915 to 1918 fighting took place on the northerly Italian Front, involving Austria-Hungary and Italy. In the Caucasus the Ottoman Empire and Russia clashed, with British and German forces also becoming involved.

In the Middle East, fighting took place in the Sinai and Palestine between British and Ottoman forces. The Mesopotamian campaign saw troops from Britain and India pitted against a chiefly Ottoman force.

The Eastern Front

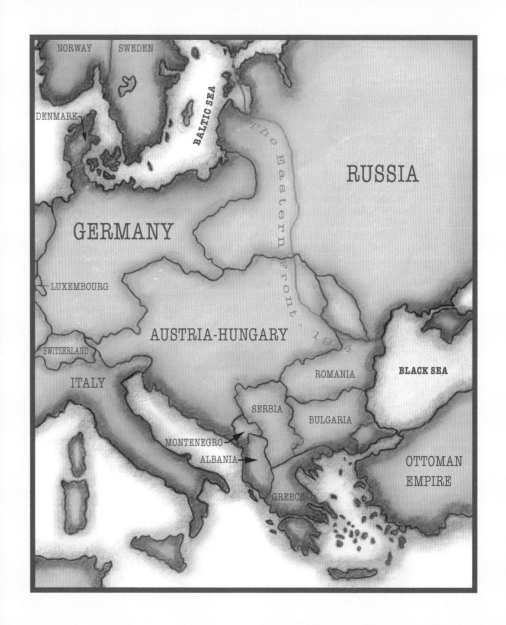

" When we marched from Kielce to the front, it seemed to me as if the world stopped where the railroad ended and the war lay in front of me, in great emptiness. Always the same picture. Simple wooden crosses along the roads, and shot up houses, still smoldering. The same tragic note repeating itself: Nothing but the lonely chimney with the stove looming up, like a sad, forsaken fellow waiting for the return of his loved ones. And a second thing is repeated every evening: the retreating Russians set fire to villages and especially bridges..."

— Peter Frenzel, 1915

The Eastern Front stretched across a distance of more than 1,600 kilometres (990 miles). The battle lines were fluid, and static trench warfare was rarely a feature of the fighting.

The opening move comprised the Russian invasions of East Prussia and the Austro-Hungarian province of Galicia in August 1914. Despite suffering defeat at the Battle of Tannenberg that month, a second Russian invasion of Galicia was more successful with Austro-Hungarian armies resoundingly routed. Germany quickly transferred forces to the east to support the beleaguered Austro-Hungarians. Fighting took place in Poland along the River Vistula, at Lodz and by the Carpathian Mountains to the year's end.

In early 1915 the east became a key strategic priority for Germany, and victory ensued for the Central Powers in the Gorlice-Tarnow Offensive in Galicia in May and at the Masurian Lakes. The Russian army was now in retreat until the German advance was halted on a line from Riga to the Romanian border at the end of the year.

Further south, the Russo-Ottoman front in the Caucasus sparked into life in early 1916, as the Russians attacked and captured Trabzon. In an effort to relieve pressure on the French at the Battle of Verdun, further Russian offensives were launched this year, including Lake Naroch (March–April) and the highly successful Brusilov Offensive in Galicia. Romania was now persuaded to join the war on the Allied side, and on August 27, Romanian troops entered Austro-Hungarian Transylvania. This provoked the Central Powers to invade Romanian territory.

The February and October revolutions in Russia in 1917 had a dramatic effect on events in the east, with Lenin's Bolshevik government attempting to halt the war. A ceasefire was declared on December 15, 1917 effectively ending fighting on the front. Peace was finally ratified with the Treaty of Brest-Litovsk in March 1918.

The Italian Front

Although nominally one of the Central Powers, Italy entered the war in May 1915 on the side of the Allies. Fighting chiefly took place against Austria-Hungary along Italy's northern border, high up in the Alps, and in successive Italian offensives at the Isonzo River, all of which failed to make progress. In the wake of the October 24, 1917 Battle of Caporetto the Italians were pushed back to the Piave River. However, at Vittorio Veneto in late 1918, a decisive Italian victory forced Austria-Hungary to surrender.

From 1915 through 1918, at least 60,000 soldiers died in avalanches: 10,000 in the "lesser" ranges of the Carnic and Julian Alps to the east, and 50,000 in the 'High' Alps – the Dolomites and the Ortier and Adamello groups – to the west.

A key feature of the Italian front was the predominantly mountainous terrain in which much of the fighting took place between 1915 and 1918. The troops of Italy and Austria-Hungary faced each other at high altitudes, often clinging precariously to steep slopes and dominating positions in an attempt to gain a tactical advantage that might dislodge the enemy.

The winters at these altitudes were harsh, and the risks of landslides, ice falls and avalanches added extra danger. Fighting took place in sub-zero temperatures for a significant part of each year, with men making use of snow trenches.

Transport in this challenging terrain proved problematic. Steep-sided river valleys provided key conduits, but road and rail links and bridges, were often non-existent. The advent of war actually encouraged the development of a transport infrastructure along the front and much building work took place. At altitude, the troops of both sides created networks of underground tunnels and shelters in the rock both for protection and to accommodate men and materiel. Heavy weapons and equipment, general stores and supplies and the sick and injured were transported by mules, cable car or hauled by soldiers across difficult sections.

" ...let me tell you that it's nearly two months now that I have been here in the front line and we suffer so I can hardly tell you. I'm in the high Cadore if you could see the snow there is still some 8 metres of snow but now the days are beginning to improve a little we have to advance... who knows how many poor Italians will have to die because they have this passion to slaughter us like sheep."
— Giovanni Procacci, 1916

Africa
and the Middle East

The wars in Africa raged around the German colonies of Kamerun, Togoland, German South-West Africa and German East Africa. Most had only recently been acquired and were not well defended, with the notable exception of German East Africa. They were also surrounded on all sides by African colonies belonging mostly to their enemies – Great Britain, France, Belgium and, later on, Portugal.

In the Middle East, conflict centred on the Ottoman Empire's circle of influence, from the straits of the Dardanelles in the north to the southern tip of the Arabian Peninsula.

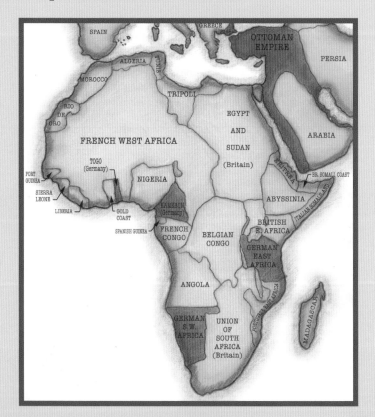

"The atmosphere was oppressive, deadly. There seemed no life in it. It was not burning hot, but held a moisture and sense of great age and exhaustion such as seemed to belong to no other place: not a passion of smells like Smyrna, Naples or Marseilles, but a feeling of long use, of exhalations of many people, of continued bath-heat and sweat. One would say that for years Jidda had not been swept through by a firm breeze: that its streets kept the air from year's end to year's end, from the day they were built for so long as houses would endure…"

— T. E. Lawrence, 1916

"Sections of Beni Ali tribesmen approached the Turkish command with an offer to surrender, if their villages be spared. Fakhri [the Turkish Pash] played with them, and in the ensuing lull in activities surrounded the Awali suburb with his troops; whom he suddenly ordered to carry it by assault and to massacre every living thing within its walls...

"...Hundreds of the inhabitants were raped and butchered, the houses fired, and living and dead alike thrown back into the flames. Fakhri and his men had served together and had learned arts of both the slow and the fast kill upon the Armenians in the North. This bitter taste of the Turkish mode of war sent a shock across Arabia; for the first rule of Arab war was that women were inviolable; the second that the lives of children too young to fight with the men were to be spared, the third, that property impossible to carry off should be left undamaged...

"...It was terribly hot - hotter than ever before I had felt in Arabia - and the anxiety and constant movement made it hard for us. Some even of the tough tribesmen broke down under the cruelty of the sun, and crawled or had to be thrown under rocks to recover in the shade. Our rifles grew so hot with sun and shooting that they seared our hands.

"We consoled ourselves with knowledge that the enemy's enclosed valley would be hotter than our open hills..."
— T. E. Lawrence, 1916

During the conflict, all of the belligerent armies recruited colonial soldiers collectively know as "Askaris" (from the Arabic word for "soldier"). Although harshly disciplined, Askaris were well paid and some were highly trained.

" Of the many plagues that beset this land of Africa not the least are the biting flies. Just as every tree and bush has thorns, so every fly has a sting. Some bite by day only, some by night, and others at all times. Even the ants have wings, and drop them in our soup as they resume their plantigrade existence once again."

— Captain Robert V. Dolbey, 1916

" In the last four weeks I had ridden 1,400 miles by camel, not sparing myself anything to advance the war; but I refused to spend a single superfluous night with the familiar vermin. I wanted a bath, and something with ice in it to drink: to change clothes, all sticking to my saddle sores in filthiness... to eat something more tractable than green dates and camel sinew..."

— T. E. Lawrence, 1917

The East African campaign comprised a series of battles and guerrilla actions, which gradually spread to portions of Mozambique, Northern Rhodesia, British East Africa, Uganda and the Belgian Congo. German colonial forces, under Paul von Lettow-Vorbeck, sought to draw Allied forces away from Europe. The Allies used a South African, Rhodesian and Indian force under Jan Smuts to confine von Lettow-Vorbeck's forces to the southern part of German East Africa.

Over 3,430 British troops were killed in action during the East African campaign, with further 6,558 killed by disease. E. Paice, in *Tip and Run: The Untold Tragedy of the Great War in Africa*, recorded approximately 22,000 British casualties in total, of whom 11,189 died. But those figures pale in comparison to native deaths. By 1917, the loss of over 90,000 African porters who had been forcibly conscripted effectively depopulated many districts. A Colonial Office official, Ludwig Boell, wrote in 1951 that the East African campaign had not become a scandal only "because the people who suffered most were the carriers – and after all, who cares about native carriers?"

" A man of importance had been shot at a place I could not pronounce in Swahili or in English, and, because of this shooting, whole countries were at war. It seemed a laborious method of retribution, but that was the way it was being done.

" A messenger came to the farm with a story to tell... It was about how the war progressed in German East Africa and about a tall young man who was killed in it... It was an ordinary story, but Kibii and I, who knew him well, thought there was no story like it, or one as sad, and we think so now.

" The young man tied his shuka on his shoulder and took his shield and his spear and went to war. He thought war was made of spears and shields and courage, and he brought them all. But they gave him a gun, so he left the spear and the shield behind and took the courage, and went where they sent him because they said this was his duty and he believed in duty.

" He took the gun and held it the way they had told him to hold it, and walked where they told him to walk, smiling a little and looking for another man to fight.

" He was shot and killed by the other man, who also believed in duty, and he was buried where he fell. It was so simple and so unimportant. But of course it meant something to Kibii and me, because the tall young man was Kibii's father and my most special friend. Arab Maina died on the field of action in the service of the King. But some said it was because he had forsaken his spear."

— Beryl Markham, *West with the Night*

The Western Front

The Western Front was the name given to the 700 km line that stretched from the North Sea to the northern border of Switzerland. In August 1914, the German Army had swept through Belgium, and by September 2 was in France and headed towards Paris. The French counter-attack resulted in the Battle of the Marne, lasting from September 4 to 10. The Germans were forced to retreat to the River Aisne and dug trenches in order to hold back the Allied advance. The Allies could not break through the trench defences and were forced to dig in as well. By the end of 1914 both armies were engaged in a deadly stalemate that would last for over three years.

"With pick and shovel we dug trenches through beautiful fields of grain, fully realising what damage we were doing to the farmers' hopes of reaping small harvests that would enable them to stem hunger during the coming winter. The patriarch with his ox-drawn plough, the matronly gleaner, and the young woman gathering grass and leaves, roots and truffles, stood arms akimbo, wordlessly, helplessly, hopelessly watching."

— Private Victor Wheeler

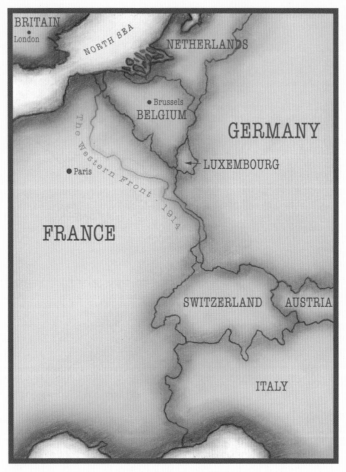

"The fortification consists of breastworks, built up high to the front, with just a little shallow trench dug behind. The reason is that drainage is so difficult. These breastworks are made of millions of tightly-made sandbags laid one upon the other, packed well together.

"Every eight yards there is a great mound of earth and sandbags strengthened by riveting, round which the trench winds. This is to localise the explosion of shells or prevent an enemy who might reach the flank being able to pour fire right down the length of a trench.

"There are communication trenches back every few yards and innumerable succeeding lines for the main army. The whole network extends in most places for three or four miles. The dug-outs are all in lines, but mostly along the communication trenches."

— John Raws, July 9, 1916

Diagram of a
Trench System

Typical Allied trench

"The war was mainly a matter of holes and ditches"

— Siegfried Sassoon, *Memoirs of an Infantry Officer*

Communication trench

Support trench

Reserve trench

Front-line trench

Deep dugout

Barbed wire

" As one can't possibly feel happy in a place where all nature has been devastated, we have done our best to improve things. First we built quite a neat causeway of logs, with a railing to it, along the bottom of the valley. Then, from a pine wood close by which had also been destroyed by shells, we dragged all the best tree-tops and stuck them upright in the ground; certainly they have no roots, but we don't expect to be here more than a month and they are sure to stay green that long."

— Lothar Dietz, 1914

Typical German trench

Aerial view of the trenches northwest of Limey, France, 1916

The Wire

After the First Battle of the Marne, wire technology (which came in several forms) was laid down extensively to trip, trap and entangle attacking troops and funnel them into kill zones. Arranged in zigzag strips or belts in No Man's Land, sometimes at knee height and sometimes much higher, wire belts could extend to hundreds of metres in depth. Wiring party duty was one of the most unpopular assignments for soldiers; steel pickets and rolls of wire had to be quietly emplaced in No Man's Land under cover of darkness.

Wire presented a formidable obstacle to any frontal attack. Artillery barrages were used to cut paths through them. Other methods for overcoming them comprised rubber mats, wire cutters, the Bangalore Torpedo (long tubes packed with explosives) and (from 1916) tanks.

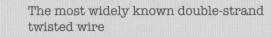

The most widely known double-strand twisted wire

Crandal zig-zag single-barb, doubled

Half-inch single-barb, twisted ribbon wire, reinforced in the centre (Thomas V. Allis patent July 26, 1881)

Half-inch double-barb, twisted ribbon wire, reinforced in the centre

Caltrops – part of the wire defensive technology and intended primarily to counter the advance of horses, mules or camels

"To give a recipe for getting a rough idea, in case you want to, I recommend the following procedure. Select a flat ten-acre field, so sited that all the surface water of the surrounding country drains into it. Now cut a zig-zag slot about four feet deep and three feet wide diagonally across, dam off as much water as you can so as to leave about one hundred yards of squelchy mud; delve out a hole at one side of the slot, then endeavour to live there for a month on bully beef and damp biscuits, whilst a friend has instructions to fire at you with his Winchester every time you put your head above the surface."

— Bruce Bairnsfather, 1914

"The next morning we gunners surveyed the dreadful scene in front of our trench... Immediately in front, and spreading left and right until hidden from view, was clear evidence that the attack had been brutally repulsed... Quite as many died on the enemy wire as on the ground. They hung there in grotesque postures. Some looked as though they were praying; they had died on their knees and the wire had prevented their fall...

"The Germans must have been reinforcing the wire for months. It was so dense that daylight could barely be seen through it. Through the glasses it looked a black mass... How did our planners imagine that Tommies, having survived all other hazards — and there were plenty in crossing No Man's Land — would get through the German wire? Who told them that artillery fire would pound such wire to pieces? Any Tommy could have told them that shell fire lifts wire up and drops it down, often in a worse tangle than before."

— George Coppard, *With a Machine Gun to Cambrai*

"My lieutenant sent me out to repair some barbed wire between our trenches and the enemy's. I went through the mist with two chaps. I was lying on my back under the obstacle when pop, out came the moon, then the Boches saw me and well! Then they broke the entanglement over my head, which fell on me and trapped me. I took my butcher's knife and hacked at it a dozen times. My companions had got back to the trench and said I was dead, so the lieutenant, in order to avenge me, ordered a volley of fire, the Boches did the same and the artillery joined in, with me bang in the middle. I got back to the trench, crawling on my stomach, with my roll of barbed wire and my rifle."

— Henri Gaudier-Brezeska, 1914

"A Fair Night Out"
Christopher J. Harvie, *If Ye Break Faith*

"It's a moonless night, a handful of figures moves slowly and quietly along the broken ground between the firing trenches. About an hour past last light they had moved from the safety of their own lines into No Man's Land through gaps in the tangle of wire, intent on getting as close as possible to the enemy lines.

"The group halts - a nervous machine gunner, some yards down the line lets off a long burst. It stops, though, the man probably chastised by an NCO for wasting ammunition. When all is quiet, the little band moves off again, getting quite near to their objective.

"Coming upon the enemy wire, a similar gap to the one they passed through is found. This could be dangerous. Moving through here would mean not having to take time cutting, and the chance of being discovered by the noise, but lanes like these are usually overwatched with machine gun teams. The patrol commander decides to work with speed and surprise as his advantage. It's a cool night, the weather has been damp for most of the week, and the line is generally quiet.

"With luck the enemy won't be too vigilant tonight. The Lewis gun team is left outside the wire to cover a quick retreat while the other four men sprint at a crouch through the obstacle. As rehearsed, once beyond they spread abreast, one each going left and right to cover the traverses, the other two dropping right into the firing bay.

"The pair of enemy soldiers in the bay are taken completely unaware. To his credit, the first one moves for his rifle and is about to shout the alarm when he is clubbed and knocked senseless. The second man, much younger, puts his hands up... He is quickly patted down and roughly man-handled out of the trench. The patrol regroups and heads back to their line, their prize in tow; all in all a fair night out."

The Stand-To

The stand-to, short for "stand-to-arms" and referred to by its Allied participants as "the morning hate", was enacted by both sides at sunrise and sunset. Experience had shown that more attacks were conducted either before dawn or after dusk, using the advantage of indistinct light, so at these times, every soldier had to stand on the trench fire step, ready to protect their trench from enemy attack.

It was a moment of highly ritualised anxiety. (The irony being, of course, that both sides would be engaged in stand-to at exactly the same time, thus negating the need for it.)

" When I halted at the edge of the trench and spied out over No Man's Land it would sometimes happen that I thought the posts holding our thin network of barbed wire were the silhouettes of a German patrol crouching there on their knees ready to rush forward. I would stare at the posts, see them move, hear their coats brushing against the ground and the sheaths of their bayonets clinking... there was nothing there – just my own anxious hallucinations."

— Rene Arnaud, *The Beauty and the Sorrow*, February 28, 1915

Artillery

Artillery developed considerably during the war, in terms of technology, tactical usage and accuracy. It dominated trench warfare, occupying an increased proportion of each force by war's end. It also caused the highest number of casualties in the fighting and the deepest fear among soldiers.

Initially artillery fire was considered vital for supporting infantry attacks, softening up enemy positions. As accuracy improved, the emphasis shifted to destroying enemy guns. Sophisticated systems of indirect fire (pioneered by the Germans) were also developed, and included spotting from aircraft, rapid communication via field telephone, and the mathematical techniques of "flash spotting" and "sound ranging".

Artillery weapons, comprising light and heavy guns and howitzers, could fire many different types of shell, including high explosive, fragmentation, smoke and poison gas shells. Further developments included new types of special anti-aircraft artillery and trench mortars.

" This is the most distressing thing about the kind of warfare we are up against here. Never a sight of the enemy, and then some fine day when a man is almost tempted to forget that he is on the front... bang! and he is carried off or mangled by a cannon fired five kilometers away. It is not glorious. The gunner has not the satisfaction of knowing that he has hit, nor the wounded at least of hitting back."

— Alan Seeger, Letter to the *New York Sun*, May 22, 1915

"How sad this death that threatens us seems! The sense of our individual impotence is heartrending. How is it possible to struggle against sovereign matter, against the tearing force that, mechanically, in a second, may scatter our bodies in tatters!

This is not the kind of war we dreamed of in August; the war of song, and of exaltation in the bright sunshine! We had hoped for epic battles and now we are going to die, pounded by scraps of iron hurled by an invisible hand; at the bottom of a hole; in the mud!"

— Andre Friborg, *The Faith of the Fighting Men*

French artillery projectiles:
420mm – 360mm – 305mm

The Dead

" We stood and sat on bodies as if they were stones or logs of wood. Nobody worried if one had its head stuck through or torn off, or had gory bones sticking out through its torn coat. And outside the trench one could see them lying in every kind of position.

There was one chap sitting in a shell-hole, with his rifle on his arm and his head bent forward, but he was holding his hands as if to protect himself, in front of his chest, in which there was a deep bayonet wound."

— August Hope, 1914

Grenades

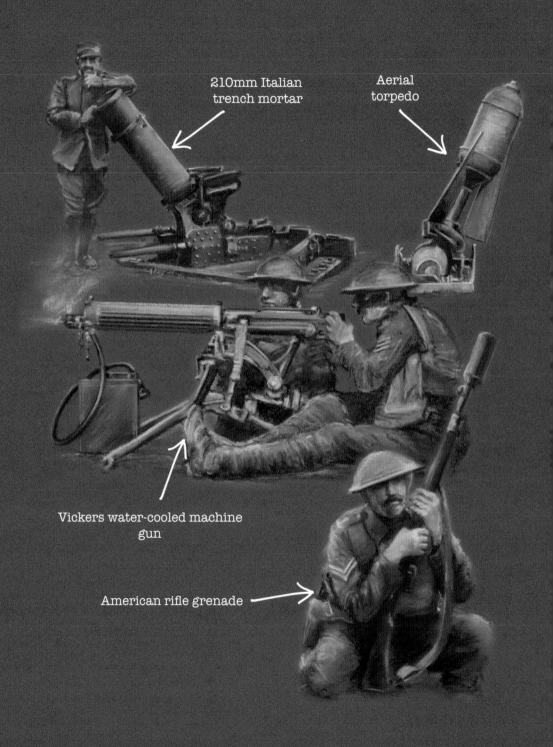

Despite initially being in short supply, the grenade played a key role in trench warfare. Bombing parties would use grenades when conducting raids on enemy trenches, tossing their lethal weapons into dugouts as they passed along an overrun trench.

Initially, Germany led the way in grenade manufacture and development, but by 1916 the Allies had caught up, with millions of improved models (notably the British "No. 5" Mills fragmentation bomb) manufactured every month. The Germans, however, would continue to develop new models, including poison gas grenades.

Grenades could be launched using a rifle attachment and a blank cartridge, or thrown by hand. They were detonated either by percussion or by timed fuse, the latter usually being activated by removing a pin from the grenade.

"There was a new terror of trench holding and dwelling. Now a man who lay down in a dugout for the night was not only in danger of being blown heavenward by a mine, or buried by the explosion of a heavy shell, or compelled to spring up in answer to the ring of a gong which announced a gas attack, but he might be awakened by the outcry of sentries who had been overpowered by the stealthy rush of the shadowy figures of the night, and while he got to his feet be killed by the burst of a bomb thrown by men whom he supposed were also fast asleep in their own quarters two or three hundred yards away."

— Frederick Palmer, *My Second Year of the War*, 1917

210mm Italian trench mortar

Aerial torpedo

Vickers water-cooled machine gun

American rifle grenade

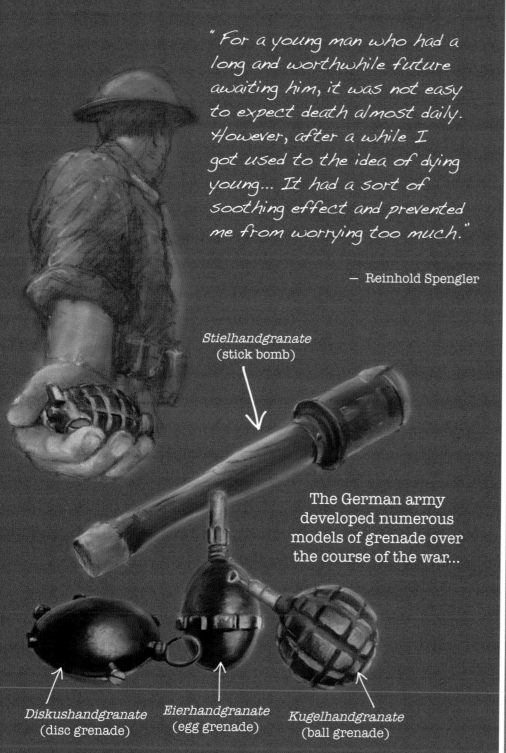

"For a young man who had a long and worthwhile future awaiting him, it was not easy to expect death almost daily. However, after a while I got used to the idea of dying young... It had a sort of soothing effect and prevented me from worrying too much."

— Reinhold Spengler

Stielhandgranate (stick bomb)

The German army developed numerous models of grenade over the course of the war...

Diskushandgranate (disc grenade)

Eierhandgranate (egg grenade)

Kugelhandgranate (ball grenade)

Snipers

"A bullet makes the merciful wound; and a bullet through the head is a simple way of going. The bad wounds come mostly from shells; but there is something about seeing anyone hit by a sniper which is more horrible. It is a cold-blooded kind of killing, more suggestive of murder, this single shot from a sharpshooter waiting as patiently as a cat for a mouse."

— Frederick Palmer, *My Year in the Great War*, 1915

Red Cross Dogs

Dogs were trained for a variety of front-line duties during the Great War, including message carrying, guard duty and pulling equipment. However, their role as first aid assistants is perhaps the most striking.

Dogs were carefully trained to enter no man's land, seek out wounded soldiers and carry medical supplies and water to them; they could also guide their handlers to any soldier unable to make his own way back to the trenches. Training took place under realistic battle conditions to desensitise the animals to noise and danger. Incredibly, these dogs could be taught to ignore dead soldiers and enemy uniforms and to freeze if a flare was sent up.

" Lieutenant von Wieland led a party of men in an attack on the Russian trenches. Seeing the task hopeless, he, wounded, sent back the men who had set out with him and lay there in the blood and muck and filth of the battlefield: The Russian fire was so murderous that no one dared bring him in.

" Presently a dark form bounded from the German trenches, rushed to Lieutenant von Wieland's side, grasped his coat between his teeth and, foot by foot, dragged him to safety. Once, but only for a moment, did he loosen his hold, and that was when a bullet creased him from shoulder to flank. The blood gushed from the wound, but the dog took a fresh hold and finished his job at the edge of the trench where willing hands lifted the lieutenant down to safety. They had to lift the dog down, too, because just then a bullet broke both his forelegs."

— T. F. Jager, Scout, *Red Cross and Army Dogs*, 1917

Horses

Horses were essential to all sides. At the outbreak of war, the cavalry was primarily considered an offensive arm, but on the Western Front at least, the effectiveness of modern weaponry saw the value of horses switch to more functional roles, such as reconnaissance and messenger duty, pulling heavy guns, transporting supplies and ferrying casualties to hospital. For the most part, the shock combat role was taken up by the tank.

There was an appallingly high equine death rate due to exhaustion, disease, artillery fire, poor weather, deep mud and front-line action. As a result the supply of horses had to be constantly replenished. The U.S.A. alone furnished half a million horses to the Allied cause between 1914 and 1917.

Procuring fodder for the vast number of horses proved challenging, particularly for Germany. The latter had relied on state-sponsored farms and annuities paid to individual horse breeders to supply equine stocks for the army, but as losses mounted, Germany faced a dire shortage of the animals.

" I remembered seeing a horse fall during the early months of the Retreat... The mem cut it hastily out of the gun-carriage harness and left it lying by the roadside, without so much as a word of regret. As we passed, I remember how its sides heaved and its eyes looked at us like the eyes of a human being being forsaken, and left to suffer and die in solitude."

— Florence Farmborough, *Nurse at the Russian Front: A Diary 1914–1918*

The Veterinary Corps

and ailments, typically battle injuries, weakness and exhaustion, mange and gas poisoning. More seriously injured animals were sent to the rear to be treated at base veterinary hospitals.

The hospitals were a great success, allowing a significant number of animals to be returned to active duty following treatment and rehabilitation. Over 2.5 million animals were treated by the corps in the course of the conflict.

Equine surgery in a French field hospital

Dogs and horses were not the only animals that served the armed forces of the Great War. More than 15 million animals were used on active duty in a variety of roles by all sides. Donkeys, mules and (in the Middle East) camels transported water, food, medical supplies, wounded men and ammunition to and from the front (there was even a British camel-mounted infantry force). Pigeons were used to ferry messages, and caged birds were kept in the European trenches to detect poison gas.

A French messenger dog recieving treatment at a mobile hospital

In the British Army, the Army Veterinary Corps (as it was then known) provided a mobile veterinary section for each division sent overseas. The section would deal with more minor issues

The Army Veterinary Corps witnessed a massive expansion in personnel between 1914 and 1918, and by war's end around 50 per cent of all British veterinary surgeons were serving in the corps.

The Memoirs of
Leonard Sebastian
U.S. Veterinary Hospital No. 8,
Claye Souilly, France

"During that time our little unit of 308 men brought fresh horses and mules to the front and then brought whatever horses and mules were wounded and fit enough to be brought back to the hospital. We would mainly travel at night and deliver about 80 horses, which was one string.

" We would bring back whatever horses could walk and those that couldn't they were killed. And anything that could not be cured in 30 days and put back into service, they were disposed of. The French bought the disposed horses and mules for 10 dollars each. I am not sure what they did with them but I guess they wanted them for things like their hides and who knows what else...

" We were not even allowed to slash their throats but we did, it was done. We could take out 2 or 3 strings of the 80 horses to a line and bring back to the hospital 50 or 60 animals. These would be horses and mules that had mostly shrapnel wounds and could be cured in 30 days or less. After the horses and mules had been in France for so long a time and because France is a wet and muddy country some of the animals would get a disease called Thrush. And I have actually see horses walk on their bone and socket and walk right out of their hooves. And then there was nothing to do but kill them..."

Cavalry...

The cavalry were ill-suited to the static trench warfare on the Western Front and many cavalry soldiers found themselves serving dismounted. In 1918, during the German Spring Offensive and the ensuing "Hundred Days", there were once more opportunities to exploit the speed and mobility of cavalry.

"*The squadron (less one troop) passed over both lines, killing many of the enemy with the sword; and wheeling about galloping on them again. Although the squadron had then lost about 70 per cent of its members, killed and wounded from rifle and machine gun fire directed on it from the front and both flanks, the enemy broke and retired.*"

— G. Flowerdew, *London Gazette*, March 1918

...vs. Tanks

" We stared aghast as slowly a tank crept toward us... We hoped the wide ditch at the side of the road would stop it. Little did we know of the capabilities of a tank! It moved to within five metres of the right section of 1st Company and stopped without firing. Now a concentrated fire from 1st and 3rd Companies was directed at the tank, hand grenades were thrown and some brave men got up and advanced from their positions. At this moment the tank tracks began to move and the tank crew opened up with a murderous machine-gun fire which was slowly directed along 1st Company trench. Those that were not killed instantly, screamed as they lay there wounded... Then the panic started."

— Feldwebel Wilhelm Speck, 1917

The tank was a new military weapon. Britain produced a prototype in late 1915 in an effort to overcome the challenging obstacles of trench warfare, and on September 15 1916 the first tank went into action at Flers-Courcelette. The value of the tank was emphatically proven at Cambrai in November 1917, where the entire British Tank Corps created a wide breach in the German lines. The French also experimented with tank design in 1916, and production began on the Schneider, although it would not enter service until April 1917. The Germans were slow to embrace the tank and by war's end had built only 20 A7V tanks. The U.S. Tank Corps adopted 200 French Renault tanks, which saw action in late 1917, and also developed its own M1917 model.

Gas Warfare

"GAS! Gas! Quick, boys! - An ecstasy of fumbling,
Fitting the clumsy helmets just in time;
But someone still was yelling out and stumbling
And floundering like a man in fire or lime. -
Dim, through the misty panes and thick green light
As under a green sea, I saw him drowning.
In all my dreams, before my helpless sight,
He plunges at me, guttering, choking, drowning."

— Wilfred Owen, "Dulce et Decorum Est", *The War Poems*

Disabling gases, such as tear and mustard gas, and more lethal gases, such as chlorine and phosgene, were widely used. Although they caused comparatively few combat deaths soldiers, understandably, lived in fear of the horrific effects of gas. Chlorine gas was first used on the Western Front by the Germans in early 1915, and by the British in September. Both sides began using mustard gas in 1917, delivered via artillery. Although only fatal in high doses, it remained active on the ground for long periods.

The Livens Projector was developed by Captain William H. Livens of the Royal Engineers. It launched a pressurised cylinder with a high content of gas over 1 km.

"The hospital is very heavy now... Sometimes in the middle of the night we have to turn people out of bed and make them sleep on the floor to make room for the more seriously ill ones who have come down from the line. We have heaps of gassed cases at present: there are 10 in this ward alone. I wish those people who write so glibly about this being a holy war, and the orators who talk so much about going on no matter how long the war lasts and what it may mean, could see a case - to say nothing of - 10 cases of mustard gas in its early stages - could see the poor things all burnt and blistered all over with great mustard-colored suppurating blisters, with blind eyes - sometimes temporally [sic], some times permanently - all sticky and stuck together, and always fighting for breath, their voices a mere whisper, saying their throats are closing and they know they will choke. The only thing one can say is that such severe cases don't last long; either they die soon or else improve - usually the former; they certainly never reach England in the state we have them here, and yet people persist in saying that God made the war, when there are such inventions of the Devil about."

— Vera Brittain, *Testament of Youth*

The Wounded

Treatment of the wounded created challenges for all sides across the theatres of the Great War. Modern weaponry inflicted terrible injuries, both physical and psychological, that needed skilled and often rapid treatment. In addition, all nations needed to establish effective systems of care to preserve levels of manpower and reduce any long-term burden on the state.

When seriously injured at the front, soldiers had to be retrieved by units of unarmed medical orderlies and officers. Operating close to the battlefield, these men demonstrated great courage in bringing casualties back, often through treacherous conditions, to the nearest field post, where first aid and assessment would take place.

If necessary, the patient would then be taken to the rear, initially by stretcher-bearer relay teams and then later by animal or wheeled transport, to be treated in a field hospital or clearing station. The more seriously wounded would be repatriated for further treatment. Preventing infection was a priority; antibiotics had not yet been developed, so cleaning and clearing wounds became a key concern.

Sickness and contagious disease (such as influenza) made up a large proportion of casualties. Doctors and nurses were warned to be on the lookout for "malingerers", who would feign illness or wound themselves to avoid the front.

"14 August – One party of stretcher-bearers was bringing down a wounded man when an airman swooped down and dropped a bomb deliberately on them. The enemy shells the stretcher-bearers all the time.

"16 August – The infantry took a few pill-boxes and a line or two of trenches from the enemy in this attack but at a fearful cost. It is only murder attempting to advance against these pill-boxes over such ground. Any number of men fall down wounded and are either smothered in the mud or drowned in the holes of water before we can reach them.

"19 August – I have had no sleep since I went on the 13th. The 109th Field Ambulance alone had over thirty casualties, killed, wounded and gassed – and this out of one hundred men who were doing the line."

— Sergeant Robert McKay, stretcher-bearer with the 109th Field Ambulance Unit, 1917

"A call came in at half-past nine to get one wounded man at Clos Bois. McConnell, driver of No.7, went with me. We neither of us had ever been there, so it was somewhat a case of the blind leading the blind. It made little difference, however, as the night was so black that nothing but an owl could have seen his own nose. We felt our way along helped by a distant thunderstorm, the flicker of cannon, and the bursting of illuminating rockets, picked up our wounded man, and were returning through Montauville when we were stopped by an officer. He had a wounded man who was dying, the man was a native of Dieulouard and wished to die there... Whether he did live or die I was never able to find out..."

— Carlyle H. Holt, "Incidents of a Driver's Life", *Friends of France, The American Ambulance Field Service*, 1916

" It didn't smell like a church anymore. Gone was the sleepy scent of waxed pews – the pews themselves having gone to make space for the cots. The lazy, dusty light tinted by the stained glass was now infused with the horror of what was happening beyond sacred walls; a rotten, unforgettable smell of weeping sores and the iron of old blood. Parishioners had been replaced by fractured men – none of whom would ever be whole again. It may not smell like a church anymore, but many inside were waiting for God.

— Christopher J. Harvie,
If Ye Break Faith

Civilian Casualties

"The resident population of the town was limited to a group of brancardiers [litter-bearers], some grave-diggers, the crews of several goulash batteries and some doctors and surgeons. I must not forget to mention the sole remaining representative of the civil population. He was an old, old man, so old it seemed the very shells respected his age... at any hour of the day or night he could be seen making his uncertain way among what were the ruins of what had been once a prosperous town - his town. With him, also tottering, was also a wizened old dog... And daily, as their town crumbled, they crumbled, until at last one morning we found the old chap dead, his dog by his side."

— Robert Whitney Imbrie at Cappy, France, March 1916, *Behind the Wheel of a War Ambulance*

"War came like a tornado, touching down in patches, taking with it one life while leaving the next person unharmed."

— James Rorimer, 1917

The numbers of civilian casualties in the Great War vary according to different estimates. Some figures exclude those who died from malnutrition and disease, while others do not. Civilian deaths might be caused by artillery or naval/air bombardment, and include the deaths of merchant seamen. It is generally accepted that there was a total of around 6 million non-combatant deaths in the course of the conflict. The Ottoman Empire lost over 2 million of its citizens, and the Russian Empire around 1.5 million. Germany, Austria-Hungary, Serbia, Romania and Italy all suffered 0.5 million deaths each. France lost 300,000 citizens, while Great Britain lost 110,000. Many other nations also lost citizens.

FINIS

"I thought of a very strange look on all faces in that camp. An incomprehensible look which a man will never see in England; nor can it be seen in any battle... It was not despair, or terror, it was more terrible than terror, for it was a blindfold look, and without expression, like a dead rabbit's. It will never be painted, and no actor will ever seize it."

— Wilfred Owen, 1917

Why did the War End?

The U.S. declaration of war on Germany and later Austria-Hungary added vital military manpower and materiel to the Allied cause.

The loss of manpower and land, and shortages of fuel and raw materials, led to increasing privation and poverty among civilian populations worldwide.

By 1917, military and civilian casualties and deaths across all nations amounted to many millions. The world was growing weary of war.

Economic blockades and falls in agricultural production saw the distribution of substitute foodstuffs. Both Russia and Turkey witnessed starving populations.

Food shortages, high prices and low civilian morale caused widespread unrest and dissent.

Dissent grew in the German High Seas Fleet in 1917. The execution of two protest ringleaders paved the way for a fleet-wide mutiny in late 1918.

REMEMBER THE LUSITANIA!

VOTES FOR WAR

WAR IS DECLARED U.S.

NEWYORK JOURNAL

House by a Vote of 373 to 50 Passes Joint Resolution

U.S. Senate

Feb.–Dec. 1916 Battle of Verdun	1917	Germany declares unrestricted submarine warfare	U.S. declares war on Germany	Chemin des Dames offensive: French troops mutiny	Bolsheviks overthrow the Russian Government	Armistice between Romania and Germany	1918 Armistice between Russia and Germany
	July–Nov. 1916 Battle of the Somme		Tsar Nicholas II abdicates				

The Fall of the Romanovs

As early as mid-1915, morale among the Russian people began to plummet. Material goods and food were in short supply, the economy was under strain, casualties were mounting from the extensive fighting, and the competence of the Imperial Army's leadership was widely questioned. This led to a series of strikes and protests among low-paid workers and unrest among the long disenfranchised peasant class.

In the wake of the February 1917 Revolution, the unpopular Tsar Nicholas II was forced to abdicate. He and his family were imprisoned, before eventually being executed by the Bolsheviks on the night of July 16–17, 1918.

March–July 1918
Germany launches four major offensives in rapid succession

November 11
Armistice goes into effect
at 11 A. M.

Kaiserschlacht

The 1918 German Spring Offensive, or *Kaiserschlacht*, was launched on March 21. It comprised a final concerted effort to break through the Allied lines on the Western Front and outflank their forces before Germany succumbed to the tightening economic blockade and American reinforcements arrived en masse.

Although the offensive made deep penetrations, the Germans were unable to move supplies and troops fast enough to keep pace with the advance of the forward elements. The offensive thus gradually ran out of steam. The Allied counter-offensive was not long in coming, and the ensuing "Hundred Days" saw the Germans yield all of the territory they had captured, before falling into headlong retreat towards the Hindenburg Line. A German surrender was now inevitable.

Armistice

" On the Fourth Army front, at two minutes to eleven, a machine-gun, about 200 yards from the leading British troops, fired off a complete belt without a pause. A single machine-gunner was then seen to stand up beside his weapon, take off his helmet, bow, and turning about walk slowly to the rear."

– Herbert Essame, November 11, 1918

On November 11, 1918, following three days of negotiation, the Armistice was signed aboard a railway carriage in the Forest of Compiègne, ending the fighting on the Western Front.

Although terms were agreed early in the morning of the 11th, when the German delegation realised the hopelessness of its position, the Armistice was to come into effect at 11 A. M. (French time). Over 2,500 men died on the last day of the war in this theatre as troops of both sides continued to fire right up to the deadline.

But the past is just the same – and War's a bloody game...
Have you forgotten yet?...
Look down, and swear by the slain of the War that you'll never forget.
– Siegfried Sassoon, *Aftermath*

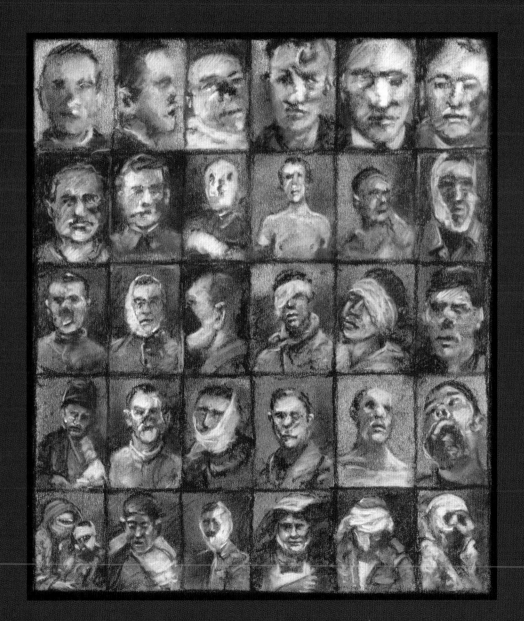

"You smug-faced crowds with kindling eye
Who cheer when soldier lads march by,
Sneak home and pray you'll never know
The hell where youth and laughter go."
– Siegfried Sassoon, *Suicide in the Trenches*

"I had climbed down from the scaffold of suffering
and returned to the world of peace and life. I
thought I was the same person I had been before...
I was wrong. I had lost my youth."

– René Arnaud, June 1916

EPILOGUE:
Christmas Eve 1914

Certain sectors of the Western Front witnessed an unofficial cessation of hostilities at Christmas 1914. On Christmas Eve – the main day of celebration for Germans – candles and trees appeared above the trenches, and carols were sung. In some sectors the men left their trenches the next day to fraternise with the enemy in No Man's Land. In others, the war continued unabated with the customary shelling and gunfire. As reports reached the high command, harsh measures were quickly put in place to discourage any future fraternisation attempts. The events of Christmas 1914 were, indeed, never to be repeated again.

" A most extraordinary thing happened... Some Germans came out and held up their hands and began to take in some of their wounded and so we ourselves immediately got out of our trenches and began bringing in our wounded also. The Germans then beckoned to us and a lot of us went over and talked to them and they helped us to bury our dead. This lasted the whole morning and I talked to several of them and I must say they seemed extraordinarily fine men.

" ...It seemed too ironical for words. There, the night before we had been having a terrific battle and the morning after, there we were smoking their cigarettes and they smoking ours."

– Lieutenant Geoffrey Heinekey

" It is a commentary on modern war that commanders should fear lest the soldiers on each side become friendly... If whole armies fraternized, politicians on both sides would be sore set to solve their problems. Yet it is possible that if there had been a truce for a fortnight on the whole trench line at any time after the Battle of the Somme the war might have ended – and what would mother have said then? "

– Colonel W. N. Nicholson,
Staff Officer Suffolk Regiment

" So Abram rose, and clave the wood, and went,
And took the fire with him, and a knife.
And as they sojourned both of them together,
Isaac the first-born spake and said,
My Father, Behold the preparations, fire and iron,
But where the lamb for this burnt-offering?
Then Abram bound the youth with belts and straps,
and builded parapets and trenches there,
And stretched forth the knife to slay his son.
When lo! an angel called him out of heaven,
Saying, Lay not thy hand upon the lad,
Neither do anything to him. Behold,
A ram, caught in a thicket by its horns;
Offer the Ram of Pride instead of him.
But the old man would not so, but slew his son,
And half the seed of Europe, one by one."

- Wilfred Owen

BIBLIOGRAPHY

Adamek, Robert J. *Pistols of World War I*, Pittsburgh, PA: Robert J. Adamek, 2001.

Aethelthryth. *Over the Front in World War 1: How Hard Can It Be to Shoot Down a Balloon?*, hubpages.com/education/Over-the-Front-World-War-1-Observation-Balloon.

ANZAC Day Commemoration Committee, Inc. *World War I: The Western Front*, www.anzacday.org.au/history/ww1/overview/west.html.

Baldridge, C. Leroy. *"I Was There", With the Yanks on the Western Front 1917-1919*, New York: G. P. Putnam's Sons, 1919.

Baxter, John. *Paris at the End of the World: The City of Light During the Great War, 1914–1918*, New York: Harper Collins, 2014.

Bean, Charles. *Digging In, Fighting Back: Hill 60, 21–28 August 1915*, www.gallipoli.gov.au/digging-in-fighting-back/hill-60-august-1915.php.

Bone, Muirhead. *The Western Front: Drawings by Muirhead Bone, Vol. 1*, New York: George H. Doran Co, 1917.

Boucher, William Ira. *An Illustrated History of World War One: The Story of World War 1 Aviation*, www.wwiaviation.com/toc.html.

Brechtelsbauer, Clemens. *Fur Kaiser und Reich: His Imperial German Majesty's U-Boats in WWI*, uboat.net/history/wwi/.

Brigham Young University Library. *The World War I Document Archive*, wwi.lib.byu.edu/.

The British Library. *Turkish Prisoners in Egypt. A report by the International Committee of the Red Cross*, www.bl.uk/collection-items/turkish-prisoners-in-egypt-report.

Bruce, George, ed. *Short Stories of the First World War*, London: Sidgwick and Jackson, 1971.

Bryant, Myffanwy. *Troopships – The Forgotten Ships of WW1*, Australian National Maritime Museum, anmm.wordpress.com/2014/02/13/troopships-ww1/ (2014).

Castle, Ian. *The Zeppelin Base Raids, Germany 1914*, Oxford: Osprey Publishing, 2011.

Colon, Raul. *The Russian Front: A Brief Look at the Imperial Air Service*, www.century-of-flight.net/ (2009).

Cornebise, Alfred E, ed. *War Diary of a Combat Artist: Captain Harry Everett Townsend*, Niwot, CO: University Press of Colorado, 1991.

The Crafton Collection, Inc. *American Etchers, Volume VIII, Kerr Eby, A. N. A.*, New York: P. & D. Colnaghi & Co.1930.

Cranston Fine Arts. *U-Boats*, www.battleships-cruisers.co.uk/u-boats.htm

Darrah, Pvt. *Samuel Herbert. Service in Siberia*, www.wwvets.com/Siberia.html.

Dawson, Coningsby. *Carry On*, London: Underwood & Underwood, 1917.

Dean, Jim W. *Some Desperate Glory... a WW1 Diary & Videos*, www.veteranstoday.com/2011/01/21/some-desperate-glory-a-wwi-diary/ (2011).

Denson, John V. *The Christmas Truce of World War I*, mises.org/library/christmas-truce-world-war-i.

DiGiulian, Tony. *United States of America Mines*, www.navweaps.com/Weapons/WAMUS_Mines.htm (2014).

Dolbey, Captain Robert V. *Sketches of the East Africa Campaign*, London: John Murray, 1918.

Duffy, Michael. *Firstworldwar.com: A Multimedia History of World War One*, www.firstworldwar.com.

English, David. *Great Aviation Quotes*, www.skygod.com/quotes/combat.html.

English Russia. *At The Eastern Front of WWI, 1914-17*, englishrussia.com/2012/05/17/at-the-eastern-front-of-wwi-1914-17/.

Englund, Peter. *The Beauty and the Sorrow: An Intimate History of the First World War*, New York: Vintage Books, 2011.

Ensminger, John. *Dog Law Reporter: Reflections on the Society of Dogs and Men, Red Cross, Iron Cross: Ambulance Dogs in World War I*, doglawreporter.blogspot.co.uk/2011/07/red-cross-iron-cross-ambulance-dogs-in.html (2011).

Eyewitness To History. *Armistice – The End of World War I, 1918*, www.eyewitnesstohistory.com (2004).

_____. *Assassination of Archduke Ferdinand, 1914* (1998).

_____. *The Battlefield Debut of the Tank, 1916* (2005).

_____. *The Beginning of Air Warfare* (2008).

_____. *The Beginning of the End of World War I, 1918* (2009).

_____. *Christmas in the Trenches, 1914* (2006).

_____. *Death of a Zeppelin, 1916* (2005).

_____. *Gas Attack, 1916* (1999).

_____. *In The American Ambulance Field Service, 1916* (2008).

_____. *Lawrence of Arabia, 1918 – Attack on a Turkish Column* (2000).

_____. *Torpedoed!, 1917* (2009).

_____. *U-Boat Attack, 1916* (1997).

Farre, Lieutenant Henry. *Sky Fighters of France: Aerial Warfare, 1914–1918*, New York: Houghton Mifflin Co., 1919.

Fitch, Willis S. *Wings in the Night: Flying the Caproni Bomber in World War I*, Nashville: Nashville Battery Press, 1989.

Forczyk, Robert. *Russian Battleship VS Japanese Battleship: Yellow Sea 1904-05*, Oxford: Osprey Publishing, 2009.

Frandsen, Bert. *Hat in the Ring: The Birth of American Air Power in the Great War*, Washington: Smithsonian Books, 2003.

Franks, Norman. *Sopwith Camel Aces of World War 1*, Oxford: Osprey Publishing, 2003.

Fribourg, Andre. *The Flaming Crucible: The Faith of the Fighting Men*, New York: The Macmillan Co, 1918.

Fromkin, David. *Europe's Last Summer: Who Started the Great War in 1914?*, New York: Alfred A. Knopf, 2004.

Fussell, Paul. *The Great War and Modern Memory*, New York: Sterling Publishing, 2009.

Galli, Richard. *Avalanche!, La Grande Guerra, The Italian Front 1915–1918*, www.worldwar1.com/itafront/avalan.htm.

Gleaves, Albert. *A History of the Transport Service*, New York: George H. Doran Co., 1921. archive.org/details/historyoftranspo00gle.

The Great War Blog. *Setting Sun: The Fate of Germany's Pacific Empire*, ww1blog.osborneink.com/?page_id=8011.

Graves, Robert. *Good-Bye To All That*, New York: Anchor Books, 1998.

The Guardian. *First World War: Inside a German trench*, www.theguardian.com/world/2008/nov/10/first-world-waetrenches-life-german

Hale, Walter. *By Motor to the Firing Line*, New York: The Century Co. 1916.

Hanson, Neil. *Unknown Soldiers: The Story of the Missing of the First World War*, New York: Vintage Books, 2005.

Hartwell, Joe. *Troopships, Battleships, Subs, Cruisers, Destroyers: A History of How the United States Navy Moved the Army to the War in Europe During WWI*, freepages.military.rootsweb.ancestry.com/~cacunithistories/ships_histories.html (2005).

Harvie, Christopher J. *If Ye Break Faith*, ifyebreakfaith.blogspot.com.

Hickman, Kennedy. *World War I: A Global Struggle, The Middle East, Mediterranean, & Africa*, militaryhistory.about.com/od/worldwarioverview/a/wwiglobal.htm.

_____. *World War I: Battle of Coronel*, militaryhistory.about.com/od/navalbattles1900today/p/Coronel.htm.

_____. *World War I: HMHS Brittanic*, militaryhistory.about.com/od/shipprofiles/p/World-War-I-Hmhs-Britannic.htm.

Histomil.com. *Re: WW1 Pictures of the Great War*, www.histomil.com/viewtopic.php?f=3&t=492&start=760.

_____. *Re: WW1 Injuries From Battle*, www.histomil.com/viewtopic.php?p=85150.

Hone, Tom. *A WWI Naval Officer's Story*, warontherocks.com/2013/09/a-wwi-naval-officers-story/ (2013).

Horn, Daniel, ed. *War, Mutiny and Revolution in the German Navy: The World War I Diary of Seaman Richard Stumpf*, New Brunswick, NJ: Rutgers University Press, 1967.

Horon, Sonia. *Animal War Heroes*, www.globalanimal.org/2012/01/08/animal-war-heroes/.

Hunt, David. *World War 1 History: Japanese Navy in the Mediterranean (2015)*, hubpages.com/education/World-War-1-History-Japanese-Navy-in-the-Mediterranean#.

Hurd, Archibald. *The Merchant Navy, Vol III*, London: John Murray, 1929. www.naval-history.net/WW1Book-MN3a-Merchant_Navy_in_WW1_Hurd.htm.

International Committee for the Red Cross. *1914–1918 Prisoners of the First World War, the ICRC Archives*, grandeguerre.icrc.org/.

Jones, Heather. *Prisoners of War*, www.bl.uk/world-war-one/articles/prisoners-of-war.

Jones, Simon. *World War I Gas Warfare Tactics and Equipment*, Oxford: Osprey Publishing, 2007.

Kiester, Edwin. *An Incomplete History of World War I*, New York: Barnes & Noble, 2007.

King-Hall, Stephen. *North Sea Diary, 1914–1918*, www.vlib.us/wwi/resources/northseadiary.html.

Kirchberger, Joe H., *The First World War, An Eyewitness History*, New York: Facts on File, Inc, 1992.

Krenzelok, Greg. *The Army Veterinary Service During the Great War, WWI*, freepages.genealogy.rootsweb.ancestry.com/~gregkrenzelok/veterinary%20corp%20in%20ww1/veterinary%20corp%20in%20ww1.html

_____. *French Army Veterinary Corps WW1*, freepages.genealogy.rootsweb.ancestry.com/~gregkrenzelok/veterinary%20corp%20in%20ww1/frenchveterinarycorpsww1.html.

_____. *Leonard Sebastian in WW1*, freepages.genealogy.rootsweb.ancestry.com/~gregkrenzelok/veterinary%20corp%20in%20ww1/Leonard%20Sebastian%20in%20WW1/Leonard%20Sebastian%20in%20WW1.htmll.

_____. *U. S. Base Hospital No. 48, Mars-Sur-Allier, Nievre, France, WW1*, freepages.genealogy.rootsweb.ancestry.com/~gregkrenzelok/basehospno48aefww1.html.

_____. *WW1 Signal Corps Pictures of the Veterinary Corps and Remount Service*, freepages.genealogy.rootsweb.ancestry.com/~gregkrenzelok/veterinary%20corp%20in%20ww1/wwisignalcorpspicturessvetcorpsremount.html.

Libby, Frederick. *Horses Don't Fly: A Memoir of World War I*, New York: Arcade Publishing, 2000.

Lynch, George. *War Wire*, babel.hathitrust.org/.

Markham, Beryl. *West with the Night*, London: Virago, 2015.

McCartney, Innes. *British Submarines of World War I*, Oxford: Osprey Publishing, 2008.

McMaster University Libraries. *Pigeon Post to Lewis Gun; Cavalry Charge to Mark VIII Tank: Evolving Technology in World War I*, pw20c.mcmaster.ca/case-study/pigeon-post-lewis-gun-cavalry-charge-mark-viii-tank-evolving-technology-world-war-i.

Memorial Gates Trust. *First World War – German East Africa*, www.mgtrust.org/gea.htm.

Memorial Hall Museum, Deerfield, MA. *Ray Elliot – 1917–1939: Ray's Early Life and His Fathers Participation in the Great War*, www.americancenturies.mass.edu/centapp/oh/story.do?shortName=elliot1917.

Mensch, Volker. *Casualties of the WW1 Airforces*, www.theaerodrome.com.

Meyer, G. J., *A World Undone, The Story of the Great War 1914–1918*, New York: Bantam Dell, 2006.

Miller, A. E. Haswell. *Vanished Armies: A record of Military Uniform Observed and Drawn in Various European Countries During the Years 1907 to 1914*, Oxford: Shire Publications, 2009.

Ministry for Culture and Heritage. *New Zealand Camel Companies*, www.nzhistory.net.nz/war/camel-corps/nz-companies.

Morris, Steven. *Grace Under Fire: First World War Soldier's Remarkable Sketches From No Man's Land*, www.theguardian.com/world/2008/oct/08/firstworldwar.heritage.

The National Archives. *First World War*, www.nationalarchives.gov.uk/first-world-war/.

The National Library of Scotland. *Pets of World War One*, www.formerdays.com/2011/03/pets-of-world-war-one.html (2011).

The National Museum. *World War One-A Maritime War, Major Naval Events in the North Sea*, www.naval-history.net/Cr03-20-00WW1-NREF.htm.

Nelson, James Carl. *The Remains of Company D: A Story of the Great War*, New York: St. Martin's Griffin, 2009.

The North American. *The War From This Side: A Third Volume*, Philadelphia: J. B. Lippincot Co., 1917.

North, Jonathan. *An Illustrated Encyclopedia of Uniforms of World War I*, Wigston, Leicestershire: Lorenz Books, 2011.

O'Neal, Mike. *World War I Fighter Pilots*, www.

usaww1.com/World_War_1_Fighter_Pilots.php4.

Ouono Design. *Dazzle Painting*, ounodesign.com/2009/01/28/dazzle-painting/ (2009).

Owen, Wilfred. *The Poems of Wilfred Owen*, Hertfordshire: Wordsworth Editions, 1994

Passion & Compassion 1914–1918. *Some WW1 German Grenades*, www.passioncompassion1418.com/decouvertes/english_grenades_all.html.

Palmer, Svetlana and Sarah Wallis, ed. *Intimate Voices From the First World War*, London: Simon & Schuster, 2003.

Persico, Joseph E. *World War I: Wasted Lives on Armistice Day*, (2006), www.historynet.com/world-war-i-wasted-lives-on-armistice-day.htm.

Pratt, George. *Murmurs: Wanderings of an Artist in the Trenches*, georgepratt.wordpress.com/2013/02/02/wwi-collection-peek/.

Pratt, George. *No Man's Land: A Postwar Sketchbook*, Northampton, MA: Tundra Publishing, Ltd., 1992.

Price, G. Ward. *The Story of the Salonica Army*, New York: Edward J. Clode, 1918. net.lib.byu.edu/estu/wwi/memoir/Salonica/salonTC.htm.

Rabjohn, R. H. *A Canadian Soldier's Diary: A Personal Series of Sketches, World War 1, 1914–1918*, Burlington, Ontario: CDM Business Services, Ltd.

Rademacher, Mary Ann, ed. *A WWI Diary: Sgt. Edgar Britton, US Army*, Enumclaw, WA: Annotation Press, 2010.

Reed, Paul. *Great War Photos*, greatwarphotos.com/.

Remarque, Erich Maria. *All Quiet on the Western Front*, New York: Ballantine Books, 1958.

Richer, William J. *Christmas in the Trenches – 1914*, www.wjpbr.com/wwixmas.html.

Roberts, Patrick. *Cats in Wartime, (2) At Sea: Ship's Cats*, www.purr-n-fur.org.uk/featuring/war02.html.

Saint-Exupery, Antoine de. *Wind, Sand and Stars*, New York: Harcourt Brace & Co, 1968.

Sassoon, Siegfried, *The War Poems of Siegfried Sassoon*, London: Faber & Faber, 2014.

Sassoon, Siegfried, *Memoirs of an Inventory Officer*, London: Faber & Faber, 2000.

Saunders, John Monk. *Wings*, New York: Grosset & Dunlap, 1927.

Saxon, Timothy. *Anglo-Japanese Naval Cooperation, 1914–1918*, (2000), Liberty University, Faculty Publications and Presentations. Paper 5, digitalcommons.liberty.edu/cgi/viewcontent.cgi?article=1004&context=hist_fac_pubs.

Silas, Ellis. *Diary of Ellis Silas*, www.gallipoli.gov.au/an-artist-at-the-landing/signaller-silas-of-the-16th-battalion.php.

Simkins, Peter, Geoffrey Jukes & Michael Hickey. *The First World War: The War to End All Wars*, Oxford: Osprey Publishing, 2003.

Smith, Gordon. *A Family that Went to War*, Australia: Gordon Smith, 2016.

Springs, Elliott White. *War Birds: The Diary of an Unknown Aviator*, London: Temple Press Books, 1966.

Stallings, Laurence. *The First World War: A Photographic History*, New York: Simon & Schuster, 1933.

Streckfuss, James. *Eyes All Over the Sky: Aerial Reconnaissance in the First World War*, Oxford: Casemate UK, 2016.

Talarico, Jessica. *The U-Boat Campaign That Almost Broke Britain*, www.iwm.org.uk/history/the-u-boat-campaign-that-almost-broke-britain.

University of California Libraries. *The War on Hospital Ships, From the Narratives of Eye-Witnesses*, London: T. Fisher Unwin, 1917, archive.org/details/waronhospitalshi00lond.

University of Oxford. *The First World War Poetry Digital Archive*, www.oucs.ox.ac.uk/ww1lit/collections.

U. S. Army Medical Department Veterinary Corps. *World War I Veterinary Hospital*,

veterinarycorps.amedd.army.mil/history/ww1/hospital.htm.

Virtual Library. *Friends of France: The American Ambulance Field Service, 1916*, www.vlib.us/medical/FriendsFrance/ff04.htm#13.

Von Richthofen, Manfred. *The Red Air Fighter*, London: Greenhill Books, 1990.

Von Und Zu Peckelsheim, Baron Spiegel. *The Adventures of the U-202: An Actual Narrative*, New York: The Century Co., 1917.

War Times Journal. *The Eastern Front: A World War One Summary*, www.richthofen.com/ww1sum2/.

Ward, Herbert. *Mr. Poilu: Notes and Sketches With The Fighting French*, London: Hodder and Stoughton, 1916.

Western Front Association. *One of the Last True Cavalry Charges: The Charge of the Dorset Yeomanry at Agagia, Western Desert, 26 February 1916*, www.westernfrontassociation.com/the-great-war/great-war-on-land/other-war-theatres/2898-one-of-the-last-true-cavalry-charges-the-charge-of-the-dorset-yeomanry-at-agagia-western-desert-26-february-1916.html#sthash.JvB087G7.dpbs.

Wheeler, O. Kieth. *Harry St Clare Wheeler, His Navy Years-World War I, 1917–1919; A Quest to Learn More About My Father*, (2007), www.wheelerfolk.org/familyphotos/hsw_ww1/his_navy_years.htm.

Whitehouse, Arch. *The Zeppelin Raiders, An Excerpt from The Years of the Sky Kings*, Award Books, 1964.

Williamson, Gordon. *U-Boats of the Kaiser's Navy*, Oxford: Osprey Publishing, 2002.

Woman's Weekly. *Freedom's Triumph: The Why, When and Where of the European Conflict*, Chicago: The Magazine Circulation Co., Inc., 1919.

Woodward, David R. *Hell in the Holy Land: World War I in the Middle East*, Lexington, KY: University Press of Kentucky, 2006.

Writer Fox. *War Poetry, 50 Poems About War, Soldier Poems*, (2014), hubpages.com/literature/WarPoems#mod_23026716.

All websites and online resources last accessed 29 March 2016.